Hidden Treasures
of the
Word of Wisdom

by
Doris T. Charriere

ISBN 0-89036-106-1

First Printing, 1978

Typesetting
by
HAWKES PUBLISHING, INC.

FRONTISPIECE

"It is true, probably, that there are many points concerning our welfare that may not have been touched upon by our Heavenly Father in the Word of Wisdom, but in my experience I have noticed that they who practice what the Lord has already given us are keenly alive to other words of wisdom and counsel that may be given.... There are a thousand ways in which we can act unwisely; our attention has been directed to some few points, and if we observe them the Lord has promised us great treasures of wisdom which will enable us to see a thousand points where we can take better care of our bodies, preserve our health, and which will enable us to train our children in the way of the Lord. The results will be that our children will be healthy and strong, and we will raise up a generation that will be a blessing to us, and through whom the Lord can accomplish His great and mighty works in the earth."

—George Q. Cannon

Journal of Discourses
Volume XII, pages 44-45

Publisher's Note: As J. Reuben Clark, Jr. would often write in the preface of his books: "For this book, I alone am responsible. It is not a church publication." The ideas of the author of **Hidden Treasures of the Word of Wisdom** are also her own, and she does not wish to imply that others must accept any of her ideas as doctrine. She only offers them for the benefit of those who are seeking further information in areas of nutrition, from one who "treasures the Word of Wisdom."

HIDDEN TREASURES
OF THE WORD OF WISDOM
TABLE OF CONTENTS

PART II

HIDDEN TREASURES
OF THE WORD OF WISDOM

Introduction

In 1833 the Lord revealed to the Prophet Joseph Smith a law of health. It was neither lengthy nor detailed like the food laws of the Jews. There were no whys and wherefores as found in the teachings of the Essenes. In fact, it was very brief and lacking in detail.

This Word of Wisdom has become one of the most widely discussed doctrines of the church. Nearly everyone who knows a Mormon knows about the restrictions in the use of tea, coffee, tobacco and alcohol; in fact, to most Mormons these restrictions **are** the Word of Wisdom. But when one prayerfully studies the Word of Wisdom, desiring to know how to apply it in his daily life, a much fuller, more beautiful concept is revealed.

At a general conference in April, 1855, Elder Ezra T. Benson (1811-1869) grandfather of present apostle, said that if a request were made for all those in the congregation to come forth who had kept the Word of Wisdom, few would come forth. But if the request were for all those who were trying to keep the Word of Wisdom, many would come forth, himself included.

He then said:

"When we first heard the revelation upon the Word of Wisdom many of us thought it consisted merely in our drinking tea and coffee, but it is not only using tea and coffee and our tobacco and whiskey, but it is every other evil which is calculated to contaminate this people. The Word of Wisdom implies to cease from adultery, to cease from all manner of excesses, and from all kinds of wickedness and abominations that are common amongst this generation—it is, strictly speaking, keeping the commandments of God, and living by every word that proceedeth from His mouth.'' (J.D. 2: 357-358)

A few years later, on April 6, 1868, Brigham Young gave these thoughts concerning the Latter-day Saints:

"I am ready to acknowledge that the Latter-day Saints are the best people, and the most willing people to do right that I know anything about. But when we take into particular and close consideration their acts, and compare them with the teachings they are constantly receiving, we think and say they are very far from taking all the counsel given them of the Lord through His servants .... When we are counseled to do that which pleases us then we are willing to obey counsel.... Again, when we consider the immensity of knowledge and wisdom and understanding pertaining to the things of this life, pertaining to the learning of this world, pertaining to that which is within our reach, and ready for the use and profit of the people, and particularly with regard to taking care of ourselves, and then consider our shortcomings, and slothfulness, we may look upon ourselves with shame-facedness because of the smallness of our attainments in the midst of so many great advantages.

"A thorough reformation is needed in regard to our eating and drinking, and on this point I will freely express myself, and shall be glad if the people will hear, believe and obey." (J.D. 12: 192)

Brigham Young and Elder Benson were addressing the saints in general conference of the church. It was their **duty** to admonish the people to obey the commandments. Although most of their emphasis was on encouraging members to cease using coffee, tea, tobacco and alcohol, nevertheless they also stressed the necessity of altering the diet to meet the standards proposed by the Lord.

This author is not in such a position. The purpose of this book is not to call people to repentance concerning the Word of Wisdom. Nor is it meant to condemn anyone, but rather to try to help those who are earnestly seeking to live the Word of Wisdom in a more positive way. It is hoped that in the relating of some personal experiences, a practical application of the counsel given in the Word of Wisdom can be demonstrated—one which is both nutritionally superior, and, in these days of spiraling food prices, more economical.

As each part of the Word of Wisdom is discussed, statements from both nutritionists and church leaders will be used to give further explanation as to how to apply these teachings. Brief mention will be given of scientific evidences which confirm these teachings. For details on these points, further study of the sources listed is suggested in the bibliography.

Since many people do not have convenient access to the complete set of the **Journal of Discourses**, references concerning the Word of Wisdom or related topics have been extracted and are included as an appendix.

It is the sincere desire of the author to avoid anything which is contradictory to church doctrine. At the same time, however, there is a desire to explore the less talked about, and more positive aspects of the Word of Wisdom. There are many points concerning health and the Lord's laws of health which are alluded to in the scriptures but are seldom referred to or discussed. These will be brought forward for your attention and consideration. Remember that the Lord does not command in all things. (D&C 58: 26-29)

It is hoped that you will enjoy exploring the many facets of the Word of Wisdom as you read this book and that you will be further inspired to study and live these teachings in a more positive way.

Chapter I

QUEST FOR HEALTH

My search for an understanding of the Word of Wisdom has been long but it has been interesting and very fruitful. It started when I had been married only a few years and had three small children. When I say small I mean both young and small in stature. It was mainly because they were such small children that two women in Relief Society kept after me with advice such as "feed your children better"—"give them more protein"—and so on and on, till I would run from Relief Society in tears and go crying to my mother. She, of course, would comfort me and tell me to ignore them. But inside I was uneasy and dissatisfied. I could explain why my children were small because neither my husband nor I are large people. He's five feet eleven inches and of medium build and if I stretch I can almost claim to be five feet three inches. So all of our children (there are now ten!) are rather small.

Even explaining that didn't relieve the feeling inside that I was not feeding my children adequately. The problem was compounded because cooking had never been numbered among my favorite hobbies. I would much rather sit at the piano and plunk out a melody for a song I was writing or get out a stack of reference books to prepare a lesson than play happy homemaker, and plan a meal. I did try to prepare good meals. To me a good meal was meat, potatoes and gravy, a cooked vegetable, and sometimes a salad if I had fresh greens. Grocery shopping was even more drudgery to me than cooking. Consequently, I seldom had on hand everything called for in a recipe. And even when by diligent effort I would plan a menu, have the necessary items on hand, and try to please my family with dessert (a rare item at our meals) something would flop. My husband would tease me by saying that I couldn't even boil water without burning it. I laugh when I think back on it now; I cried at the time.

In fact, I cried a lot then. With three pre-schoolers at home I could never seem to keep up with things. But possibly one of the most frustrating things was a condition I had which was similar to epilepsy, but wasn't epilepsy. I first became aware of it before my first child was born. I would have spells of faintness and loss of balance and at times my arms or legs would jerk convulsively. My trips to doctors began at that time and continued off and on for the next 18 years. The "spells" took on all kinds of variations which challenged my ability to describe them to the doctors. But always there was a diagnosis such as, "Your symptoms aren't typical." It turned out my symptoms weren't typical of anything. But they were very frustrating.

At that time my sister was becoming a "food fanatic" and she tried to tell me my problem was nutritional. She also thought my children needed better nutrition. I balked for a while, but she finally got me to read a couple of good books on nutrition and good nutrition finally started making sense to me. My fourth child was my "brewer's yeast" baby, and what a beautiful, healthy baby. And I was actually able to nurse him. What a joy!

So I learned a little about how to be healthier and to have healthier children. But I still blacked out and I kept adding new symptoms to my "spells," and my purpose in studying nutrition has been to help me get over these "spells." I have kept trying and I have kept studying, and I think this is what the Lord intended.

CHART

Section 89

Revelation	Revelation given through Joseph Smith the Prophet, at Kirtland, Ohio, February 27, 1833, known as

THE WORD OF WISDOM

Word of Wisdom	1. A Word of Wisdom, for the benefit of the council of high priests, assembled in Kirtland, and the church, and also the saints in Zion—
Will of God	2. To be sent greeting; not by commandment or constraint, but by revelation and the word of wisdom, showing forth the order and will of God in the temporal salvation of all saints in the last days—
Principle with Promise	3. Given for a principle with promise, adapted to the capacity of the weak and the weakest of all saints, who are or can be called saints.
Evils and Designs	4. Behold, verily, thus saith the Lord unto you: In consequence of evils and designs which do and will exist in the hearts of conspiring men in the last days, I have warned you, and forewarn you, by giving unto you this word of wisdom by revelation—
Strong Drink	5. That inasmuch as any man drinketh wine or strong drink among you, behold it is not good, neither meet in the sight of your Father, only in assembling yourselves together to offer up your sacraments before him.
	6. And, behold, this should be wine, yea, pure wine of the grape of the vine, of your own make.
For Washing Body	7. And again, strong drinks are not for the belly, but for the washing of your bodies.
Tobacco	8. And again, tobacco is not for the body, neither for the belly, and is not good for man, but is an herb for bruises and all sick cattle, to be used with judgment and skill.

Hot Drinks	9. And again, hot drinks are not for the body or belly.
Wholesome Herbs	10. And again, verily I say unto you, all wholesome herbs God hath ordained for the constitution, nature, and use of man—
In Season	11. Every herb in the season thereof, and every fruit in the season thereof; all these to be used with prudence and thanksgiving.
Meat Sparingly	12. Yea, flesh also of beasts and of the fowls of the air, I, the Lord, have ordained for the use of man with thanksgiving; nevertheless they are to be used sparingly;
Pleasing Unto Me	13. And it is pleasing unto me that they should not be used, only in times of winter, or of cold, or famine.
Staff of Life	14. All grain is ordained for the use of man and of beasts, to be the staff of life, not only for man but for the beasts of the field, and the fowls of heaven, and all wild animals that run or creep on the earth.
Use in Famine	15. And these hath God made for the use of man only in times of famine and excess of hunger.
Grain and Fruit	16. All grain is good for the food of man; as also the fruit of the vine; that which yieldeth fruit, whether in the ground or above the ground—
Wheat for Man	17. Nevertheless, wheat for man, and corn for the ox, and oats for the horse, and rye for the fowls and for swine, and for all beasts of the field, and barley for all useful animals, and for mild drinks, as also other grain.
Walking in Obedience	18. And all saints who remember to keep and do these sayings, walking in obedience to the commandments, shall receive health in their navel and marrow to their bones;
Treasures of Knowledge	19. And shall find wisdom and great treasures of knowledge, even hidden treasures;
Run and Not Be Weary	20. And shall run and not be weary, and shall walk and not faint
The Promise	21. And I, the Lord, give unto them a promise, that the destroying angel shall pass by them, as the children of Israel, and not slay them. Amen.

Chapter II

HOW DO WE
PRACTICE THE PRINCIPLE?

"A Word of Wisdom, for the benefit of the council of high priests, assembled in Kirtland, and the church, and also the saints in Zion—To be sent greeting; not by commandment or constraint, but by revelation and the word of wisdom, showing forth the order and will of God in the temporal salvation of all saints in the last days." (D&C 89: 1-2)

The Lord said, "not by commandment or constraint." Why was the Word of Wisdom not given as a commandment? In the Doctrine and Covenants, 29: 34-35, the Lord says He has never given a temporal commandment. Man is to be an agent unto himself. (Moses 6: 56) The Lord will reveal His will or tell what the order of things should be and then man has his agency to decide whether or not to abide by these words of wisdom.

Stephen R. Covey, author of **Spiritual Roots of Human Relations**, says the church does not designate practices—it teaches principles. Joseph Smith said, "I teach them correct principles and they govern themselves." Doctrine and Covenants 89: 3 states that the Word of Wisdom is given for a principle—with promise. The principle is given in verses 5 through 17. The promise is given in verses 18 through 21. Nowhere in section 89 are we told how to practice this principle. This is for each one of us to work out for ourselves. We are each at different levels in our progress. Dr. Covey compares our steps of progress to the genesis account of creation. The Lord created the earth in six days, or six creative periods. These creative periods followed in logical, sequential order, one after another. We should use much the same pattern as we strive to improve. Thus we would go through Day One, Day Two, and so on (our creative periods) in their proper order. We learn line upon line, precept upon precept. We grow inch by inch and day by day. So each must practice a principle at his own level.

This is certainly true in relation to the Word of Wisdom. Look at the Word of Wisdom in the light of a "Day One, Day Two" system of progress. The following chart suggests how these different "days" might be represented. The days are hypothetical and may vary for each individual.

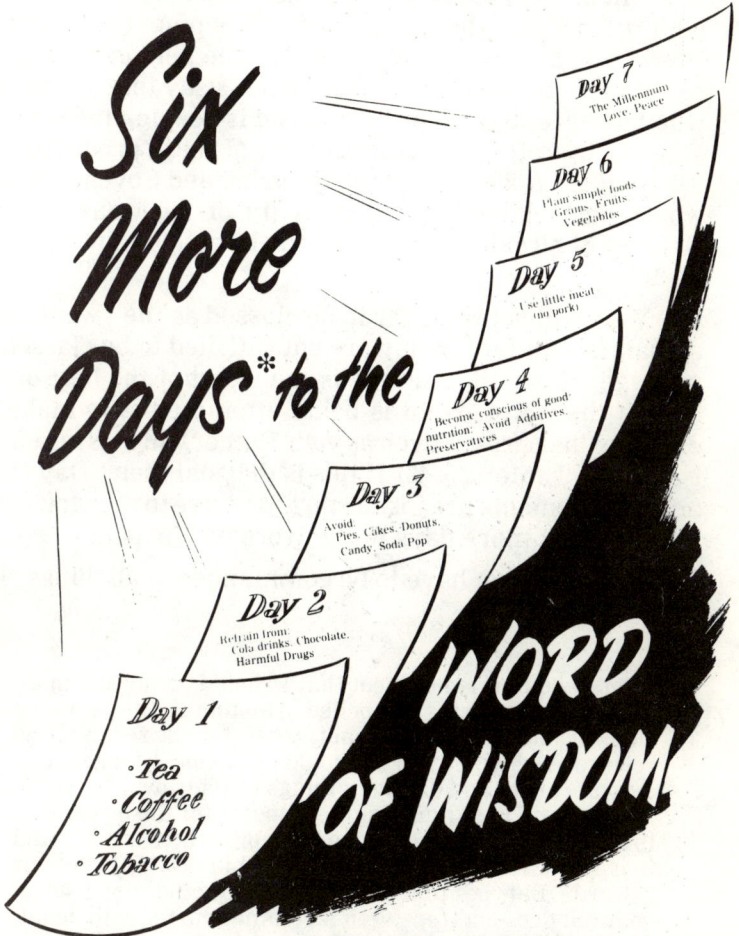

*The days are hypothetical and may vary for each individual.

Although the Word of Wisdom was not given as a commandment, it was nevertheless accepted as binding on the saints at the general conference September 9, 1851.[1] Therefore a member must now be keeping the Word of Wisdom in order to get a temple recommend, be baptized, or be ordained to the priesthood. "Keeping the Word of Wisdom" has always indicated that the person did not use tea, coffee, tobacco or alcohol. So let's say that the person who has accepted this principle and is keeping the Word of Wisdom by refraining from the use of these products is at "Day One." According to the Doctrine and Covenants, this would be "adapted to the capacity of the weak and the weakest of all saints who are or can be called saints." (D&C 89: 3)

Most will not be eager to be classed as the "weakest of all saints." In fact, many are not satisfied to be classed as average. After all, average is the worst of the best or the best of the worst. What is being attempted is to make an effort to "be perfect, even as your Father which is in heaven is perfect." (Matt. 5: 48) If this is the goal then "Day One" accomplishments are just a start. We have to recognize that there are **six more days** to the Word of Wisdom.

We should not have to be commanded in all things. The Lord has said:

> "For behold, it is not meet that I should command in all things; for he that is compelled in all things, the same is a slothful and not a wise servant; wherefore he receiveth no reward. Verily I say, men should be anxiously engaged in a good cause, and do many things of their own free will, and bring to pass much righteousness; for the power is in them, wherein they are agents unto themselves. And inasmuch as men do good they shall in nowise lose their reward. But he that doeth not anything until he is commanded, and receiveth a commandment with doubtful heart, and keepeth it with slothfulness, the same is damned." (D&C 58: 26-29)

As we progress in the gospel we have the desire to more fully keep the commandments, not just the letter of the law but also the spirit of the law. With this determination we consider seriously whether there are not other substances which are also harmful to our bodies, things which could hinder our temporal salvation. What other things have "evil and conspiring men" devised? At "Day Two" a person would be going against his conscience if he drank cokes,[2] hot chocolate,[3] or used harmful drugs. He would question whether he should eat so much meat. He knows that overeating and being a glutton is not in keeping with the spirit of the law.

When a person gets to "Day Three" he begins to wonder if what he had considered well-balanced meals are really what the Lord had in mind when He gave the Word of Wisdom. When the Lord said to use meat sparingly did He mean a quarter of a pound of meat per person two or three times a day? Is spaghetti and white bread the way he intended man to use grain? Did He really mean fruits in season or is it permissible to use canned fruits and vegetables? Just what did He mean? At "Day Three" many questions arise. Where do you find the answers? We have been counseled to accept the truth wherever it may be found. We are told to "seek ... out of the best books words of wisdom; seek learning, even by study and also by faith." (D&C 88: 118) So at "Day Three" we begin to study.

After much study and effort toward improvement we rest uneasily at "Day Four." We are uneasy because some of the newfound "facts" are contradicting each other. But we nevertheless feel very strongly that we are on the right track.

It is confusing when the National Dairy Council says, "Everybody needs milk," a chiropractor says nobody over nine years of age needs milk, and Adelle Davis says that milk is a must but it should be raw, and certified. One writer says vinegar and honey will cure all ills and still another writer says vinegar is not good for the stomach.

But through all the confusion some points are clear. For instance, white flour and white sugar products do not contribute to good health. Vitamins and minerals are essential. A diet which includes whole grains, fresh fruits, and raw vegetables is preferable to a diet of refined foods.

At Day Four we might also re-examine the phrase "hot drinks are not for the body or the belly." (D&C 89: 9) Though the prophets have stated that the hot drinks referred to are tea and coffee, nevertheless no drink should be served too hot (or icy cold) as this is damaging to the stomach.

At Day Five frustration is replaced by peace of mind as the blessing is offered upon the food placed before us. With full faith and sincerity we ask that "this food be blessed to nourish and strengthen our bodies." No longer is there the feeling of hypocrisy that sometimes occurs from offering such a blessing over a meal of "foodless" foods which we know are not really able to give the body proper nourishment.

At Day Five the words of Brigham Young finally reach listening ears. His repeated counsel to the saints of his day to cease eating pork[4] and fat meat and to not let children eat meat[5] makes sense. You can finally accept the fact that the Lord prefers meat to be used only in critical times such as famine or the cold of winter. Day Five is where you further break from traditional eating habits and adhere to practices which allow the best digestion of food, such as not eating major starches and proteins at the same meal.[6]_[7] Cooking takes a back seat and you enjoy the freedom and joy of eating nearly all food in its natural form. Day Five is transitional point.

Chapter III

AWAKENING TO DAY SIX

I caught a glimpse of Day Six one beautiful morning while I was in Southern California. I was sitting in the sunshine in front of my cottage, reading some material written by the doctor I had gone so far to see. It was beautiful. The sunshine was warm, the scenery was serene, and the words I was reading were inspiring—and so full of truth. I was filled with such a tremendous sensation when suddenly it burst into my mind and my heart: "This is the Word of Wisdom. This is how it's supposed to be. This is what I've been praying for!"

I had come to see this health doctor as a last resort. My spells had increased to the point that I was down in bed about four days out of every week. I could never tell when a spell would come on me. It might be while I was fixing supper, in the middle of choir practice, as I sat in the doctor's waiting room or even as I lay in bed. Many times I had been administered to by my husband or others holding the priesthood and had received immediate relief, but later the condition would return. I am convinced the Lord used this affliction to lead me to further truths.

As my spells increased in frequency and interfered more and more with my regular activities a friend urged me to see a doctor. Somewhere there had to be an answer. But I had already seen doctor after doctor and had never received any help. The only doctor I would even consider seeing was in Southern California. I had been told he had a different method of diagnosis. At my friend's urging I agreed to go to California to see if he could help.

The evening I arrived the doctor was giving a lecture. He said that our bodies, when given the right food and exercise, and effective mental and spiritual stimulation, can give us a lifetime of joy, service and success. He spoke of God's natural laws of health, of fresh fruits and vegetables, of whole-grain cereals, and of clean fresh air, and pure water. He told of the healing and tranquilizing qualities of color and of the effects of music.

As I left the lecture hall I felt as though I was seeing this world in a new light. It can offer us that which is fresh, clean, natural and beautiful. By learning to understand the natural laws of God we learn to appreciate these things he placed here on earth for our health and well-being. I thought to myself that even if the doctor could not diagnose my condition, it had been worth the effort just to see the possibilities of this new way of life.

The doctor analyzed my situation and said: "I feel that your body under natural circumstances knows best how to perform its duties and I think it is only our 'civilized' activities and our man-made ideas that get us into trouble. I believe that good health is the greatest prevention of disease. What I do is to try to bring things back to natural as much as possible. So let's work on improving the health of the body." He then proceeded to outline a program of exercise and diet to help accomplish this task.

As I returned home I still had to face the uncertainty of not knowing when another "spell" would hit me. But a great blessing came to me as I was able to confidently teach my children the right way to live—a full, rounded life of good health through nutritious food, regular exercise, fresh air, pure water, a happy attitude, good friends and love of God and His wonderful laws designed for our health and happiness.

My visit to the health doctor not only helped me a great deal physically, but it opened new horizons to my understanding about my body and how I could be involved in increasing my health and vitality.

This opened the door to Day Six for me and let me see the possibilities that lie in the future if I diligently seek to live all these rules of good health.

Chapter IV

HOW FAR TO EDEN?

What does Day Seven represent? It represents the ultimate in obedience to the Word of Wisdom—living to the fullest this and every other instruction which the Lord has given with respect to health. Doing so brings the total blessings of the promise. This will be as it was practiced in the Garden of Eden and will again be practiced during the Millennium. Diet will consist of fruits and a little simple food, according to Brigham Young. (J.D. 12: 37) Life will be spent walking in obedience to all the commandments. Hearts will be full of love and peace. It represents the ideal, or the ultimate in perfection for this earth life.

Where are you? Prof. Covey says we cannot jump from Day One to Day Six and skip Days Two through Five. This applies whether we are learning new skills, working to overcome our weaknesses, improving communications with our teenagers, or living a gospel principle. Are you still at Day One or are you working to overcome the problems of Day Two? Are you ready to begin studying at Day Three? Often the motivation to study occurs only after a situation has arisen which makes it imperative that one learns how to maintain the health he has or to improve it to survive and live.

Oh, to skip Day Four! Because of its frustrations and confusion, Day Four is for many the most difficult. Perhaps with a picture of what lies ahead in Days Five and Six you could avoid much of the confusion found in Day Four. The basic step in Day Four is the learning process. You should study nutrition so that you can understand how the simple foods recommended as our ultimate diet can actually provide all the nutrients necessary for excellent health. It is also faith promoting to meet or to study the words of the many people who are trying to find the right program for optimum health. It also strengthens one's faith to know he has a standard to hold to, to be kept from being "tossed to and fro by every wind of doctrine." (Ephesians 4: 14) This standard is the Word of Wisdom.

Caution should be exercised to avoid "helping" others who are not ready or willing to practice this health principle at such a level. As Bruce R. McConkie mentions in his book, **Mormon Doctrine** (pg. 845, second edition), some people become cranks with reference to this law of health. **One should use the Word of Wisdom as a guide to health. He should not use it as a scale to judge another.**

So we must recognize where we are now, set our goals, both long-range and immediate, and start to study and then practice what we learn. Until eating habits and other practices are perfect, there is still need of repentance. Can such a state of perfection be reached on this earth at this time? It is doubtful. We have been careless in our stewardships. We have allowed the air, water and soil to become polluted. This has affected the quality of our food. We have also inherited weaknesses from our parents, to the third and fourth generations, as the Lord said (Mosiah 13: 13). But we can seek for the best that is available to us and gain as much as we can. To recognize that which is better, and begin to change, is repentance.

Just as with other points of the gospel, it will take constant, diligent effort to overcome bad habits, throw off harmful traditions, and seek for that which is best. Each of us has the privilege of the guidance of the Holy Ghost to help in understanding the Word of Wisdom and its practical application in our lives. The Word of Wisdom can be adapted to the weakest and yet offer a challenge to the strongest.

Health

Barriers to good health

Chapter V

EVILS OF CONSPIRING MEN

"Behold, verily, thus saith the Lord unto you: In consequence of evils and designs which do and will exist in the hearts of conspiring men in the last days, I have warned you, and forewarn you, by giving unto you this word of wisdom by revelation—" (D&C 89: 4)

The Lord's stated purpose in revealing the word of wisdom was to give warning of evils and designs of conspiring men. One need only read the daily paper to see examples of many evils: fraud, robbery, murder, bribery and every other conceivable crime. These crimes are easily recognized and need no revelation of warning from the Lord. The evils and designs of which He wished to warn us were of a more deceptive nature. At the time the revelation was given, the specific items He designated (tobacco, strong drink, hot drinks) were in common use and there was no scientific evidence that they were especially harmful. It has taken many years of urging by our prophets and leaders to convince the general body of the saints to avoid the use of these forbidden articles. In our day the scientific evidence of the harmfulness of these substances is so well known that it is foolish for anyone to use them. In spite of this there are billions of dollars a year spent on these things.

This is mute evidence of the success which is being enjoyed by evil and conspiring men in these last days. Their number-one design is to gain wealth. From their fortunes, they expend vast sums in advertising to increase their markets and equally vast sums in other ways to protect these markets. In spite of the proven dangers from such products, the governmental agencies which have been set up to protect the consumer have done little until forced to by public pressure. Even under pressure their efforts have been insignificant. Yet these same agencies have restricted the use of certain vitamin supplements under the guise of protecting the consumer from wasting his money on needless items. It is ironic to consider that a person can buy as much beer, cigarettes, coffee, and tea as he wants and yet is restricted to 10,000 milligrams of Vitamin A and 400 units of Vitamin D.

Evil and designing men make vast fortunes from the sale of harmful products. Other conspiring men can weaken a nation by destroying or withholding health-giving products. The Lord has warned us of these things. It is up to us to obey His counsel and protect ourselves.

The first warning the Lord issued concerned strong drinks. "...Inasmuch as any man drinketh wine or strong drink among you, behold it is not good, neither meet in the sight of your Father." (D&C 89: 5) The Lord clearly states that wine or strong drink is not good for man and is not acceptable in the sight of the Lord. To an ever-loving Father in Heaven, who is concerned for our eternal happiness, who watches over us as we sojourn here on earth, it must be a sad sight indeed to see His children wallowing in the miseries brought on by drinking: the scarred and mangled bodies pulled from automobile accidents—the victims of drunken drivers, the wife who is beaten by her drunken husband, the children who go hungry because the paycheck has been squandered on booze, the wino wandering along skid row.

Brigham Young preached for years on the evils of tea, coffee, alcohol and tobacco. During one discourse he said he could tolerate the use of tea or coffee "because they do not kill a man outright, but whiskey makes a dog of him at once .... Tobacco is bad enough; its excessive use will shorten a man's life about ten years, but whiskey degrades him far lower than the brutes."

There are many people who class themselves as social drinkers and feel they are being quite temperate. They are really in no position to judge themselves. Even a few drinks alter a person's behavioral patterns and can be a source of embarrassment to family or friends. The drinker may even be unaware of the change in himself. A "social drinker" may be playing Russian roulette. There is a margin of only one drink which separates the social drinker from the alcoholic and one never knows which drink that may be.

In the old days of the temperance marches the cry was "It's the tool of Satan!" There can be no question that this is a true statement. Everything associated with drinking comes under Satan's realm: The wasted money which could otherwise have gone for a worthwhile cause, the lowering of morals, the increase of crime, and the total degradation of the drinker. What greater prize could Satan desire?

For those who have fallen prey to this habit, total abstinence is the best answer. To aid the body through this crisis, all of the nutritional elements should be supplied in abundance. Several studies have been done which show the benefits of taking large quantities of the B complex vitamins, with particular emphasis on niacinamide, in controlling alcoholism. This is a reasonable therapy, as drinking destroys the B vitamins and causes damage to the nerves. Vitamin C is also recommended as it is needed to detoxify the poisons in the system acquired through drinking.

As usual, prevention is far easier than cure. The Lord has counseled His Saints to not use wine or strong drink as He desires them to enjoy health and happiness and be worthy servants to carry on His work.

Wine was used in the sacrament in biblical days and again when this ordinance was restored in these last days. While warning about the use of wine or strong drink the Lord signifies its use as being appropriate "only in assembling yourselves together to offer up your sacraments before

Him. And behold, this should be wine, yea, pure wine of the
grape of the vine, of your own make.'' (D&C 89: 5,6) In
essence this wine is pure, unfermented grape juice. In the
Doctrine and Covenants 27: 1-4 He cautions the saints to not
purchase wine or strong drink from their enemies for use in
the sacrament but to use "wine made new among you.'' He
further says it doesn't need to be wine. Therefore, at the
present time water is used in the sacrament.

"And again, strong drinks are not for the belly, but for
the washing of your bodies.'' (D&C 89: 7) The use of alcohol
as a wash for the body is a well-accepted practice. It can be
used to cool a patient with a high fever. It can be used as a
disinfectant. It can be used as a cooling, soothing foot wash.
But it is not to be used as a drink.

"And again, tobacco is not for the body, neither for the
belly, and is not good for man, but is an herb for bruises and
all sick cattle, to be used with judgment and skill.'' (D&C
89: 8)

As chief health officer of the United States, a surgeon
general said the country should portray cigarette smoking
"as what it really is—a dirty, smelly, foul, chronic form of
suicide.'' If this description of cigarette smoking is true,
why do so many people smoke? To quip "The devil made me
do it'' would be a very reasonable answer, for in Moroni 7: 12
we are told the devil "inviteth and enticeth to sin'' and "is an
enemy to God and fighteth against Him continually.''

The devil's reward for enticing man to smoke cigarettes
is well worth his efforts. His first reward is that man
becomes disobedient to the Lord's direct counsel that
"tobacco is not for the body, neither for the belly.'' The man
who smokes is therefore choosing to serve Satan rather than
the Lord.

His second reward is the satisfaction of claiming
another slave. This comes a very short time after a person
starts smoking. It takes comparatively few cigarettes to
create an addiction because of their high nicotine content. It

has been claimed that a safe cigarette is entirely feasible—one made from strains of tobacco containing little or no nicotine which, when combined with a high filtration system, would eliminate the dangers of smoking. But if the addiction factor were eliminated, it is quite obvious what **would happen** to the volume of tobacco sales. Would a tobacco company doing a lucrative business be willing to risk losing sales simply to save lives?''

That is the devil's third and grandest reward—to bring misery and death to millions of God's children. Nicotine is the most deadly of the poisonous substances found in cigarettes. If one drop of nicotine were injected into the body it would cause instant death. This would perhaps be a more humane death than that which ultimately comes from smoking cigarettes.

There are hundreds of thousands of deaths per year in the United States which are directly attributable to cigarette smoking. These include deaths from brain tumors, lung cancer, heart failure and emphysema.

Suicide is not an infrequent result of cigarette smoking. A young married couple talked to their doctor, asking him, as a doctor, what he thought about cigarette smoking. His reply was to the effect that any doctor knows smoking is harmful to the body. He was then asked—in light of this statement—why did he smoke? He said, ''We all have our vices and that is one of mine. We are going to die one way or another sometime so what does it matter?'' A few years later he learned he was going to die of cancer and chose suicide instead.

Besides the nicotine in cigarettes, there are also at least seven cancer-producing agents and from fifteen to twenty other irritating or poisonous substances including hydrogen cyanide and carbon monoxide. Cigarettes are not the only harmful form of smoking. Whether tobacco is used in pipes, cigars, snuffed or chewed, the poisons are still getting into the body. To discontinue cigarettes and substitute the pipe or cigar is pure folly. In tobacco the devil has a fully loaded weapon of destruction regardless of the form in which it is used.

The best defense against such a weapon is to resist the temptation in the first place. Whether it be alluring commercials or social pressure of friends, such temptations can be thwarted if you have a firm determination to never take a cigarette. If you are already a slave of the cigarette habit, it takes great effort to overcome this addiction, but with a firm conviction that this is what you should do, it can be done. Heavy supplements of Vitamin C and the B vitamins can be helpful in detoxifying the poison in your system which causes the physical craving for tobacco. All of the other essential nutrients should be supplied in abundance to help your body repair the damage which has been done.

Again, tobacco is not for the body, neither for the belly ... but is an herb for bruises and sick cattle. It has its use. Beware of its misuse.

"And again, hot drinks are not for the body or belly." (D&C 89:9)

Often when persons are investigating the church and hear the Word of Wisdom they comment that they would have no problem giving up drinking and it would be a blessing to quit smoking, but how could they live without coffee? The question might be reversed and be, "How long can you live with it?"

More and more reports are showing the harmful effects of coffee. For people with glaucoma even a single cup of coffee can increase intraocular tension; many cups can bring on a violent glaucoma attack. Those with heart disease should know that one cup of coffee, which acts as a stress, causes a prompt rise in blood fats and cholesterol; many cups triple the level. Ulcer patients are told to stop drinking coffee (as well as alcohol and tea) because it increases the stomach acids which irritate the ulcers.

Strong coffee given to rats and dogs caused loss and graying of hair, convulsions, paralysis, watering eyes, and many more symptoms, none of which occurred in animals receiving decaffeinated coffee.

There are some members of the church who still use these forbidden items. Their lack of obedience is not because they do not understand the harmfulness of these things; it is because they cannot discipline themselves enough to break the habit.

The saddest result of this is that the offender is not entitled to the full influence of the Holy Ghost. (J.D. 15: 195) It is harder for these people to comprehend things of a spiritual nature. Their goals are much lower because they cannot comprehend the glory of the higher goals.

A woman who was active in church, busy with genealogy and kind and generous felt she needed her cup of tea to relax her nerves. In defense of this offense she said tea wasn't that harmful and if she ever felt it was hindering her progress she would stop using it. Her husband was a nonmember so she was unable to go to the temple so it really didn't seem to matter if she had her cup of tea or not.

What she was not aware of, but what was visible to others, was her inability to fully accept other church doctrines or the higher goals. When different requirements of Celestial law were discussed she would counter, "No one says you have to aim for the Celestial Kingdom. We're told that the Terrestrial world is far beyond anything we can imagine." We assumed she was rationalizing on this point because it seemed doubtful to her that her husband would ever join the church and she had resigned herself to being with him in the Terrestrial world.

But when he passed away and she was free to apply for a temple recommend and receive her endowments, she didn't. Time passed and she still didn't make the effort. Friends and family who urged her to give up her tea met with the same old answer, "A little tea doesn't hurt—it calms my nerves." Finally a wonderful home teacher, who was also her bishop, was able to persuade her to give up her tea. In a very short time her outlook changed, she became active in temple work and she began to comprehend the higher laws of God.

The tea had not affected her mind or body nearly as much as it had her spirit.

The four major items in the Word of Wisdom are generally considered to be the negative parts of the Word of Wisdom. However, there are many other substances which have bad effects on our body. Common sense must be applied.

Chapter VI

ALL WHOLESOME HERBS

"...All wholesome herbs God hath ordained for the constitution, nature, and use of man ..." When we think of herbs we usually think of things such as parsley, marjoram, basil, and thyme. But until relatively recent times, herbs referred to almost all varieties of the vegetable kingdom. In fact the definition of herb is a plant which has a soft stem, which dies down to the ground each year. This distinguishes the herb from the shrub or tree. So with this definition, many of the vegetables we commonly eat are classified as herbs.

"...All wholesome herbs" are for the "**constitution, nature,** and **use** of man." You have heard of a person who has a strong constitution, one who stands his ground in the face of adversity or confrontation and holds firmly to his beliefs. On the other hand, a person with a weak constitution is more like putty and unable to hold his own or stand up under pressure. Constitution also refers to the physical makeup of your body. Here the Lord says that **wholesome herbs** are for building the constitution of man.

They are also for the **nature** of man. Now the nature of man is different from the nature of either plants or animals. We cannot dig our toes into the earth and lift our arms up into the sunshine and get proper nourishment. Our system is programmed to use the food which has already been prepared for us. That is, the plants gather their nutrients from the soil, air and light and through the process of photosynthesis develop the chlorophyll which is in a perfect form to nourish our bodies.

And likewise our system is not like that of the carnivorous animal. The animal gobbles down hunks of meat without chewing it up or mixing it with saliva. Saliva does not help digest meat. In fact, it hinders its digestion. It is the stomach juices which digest the meat.[1] But meat doesn't stay in the stomach long enough to be completely digested. It passes on to the intestines. Now a dog or other carnivorous animal has a very short intestinal tract and the left-over undigested meat soon passes out of the body. But when man eats meat, first he cooks it, then he chews it thoroughly mixing the saliva into it. When it reaches the stomach the saliva neutralizes the stomach juices which could have at least helped digest it. It passes on into the intestinal tract, which curls around and around and, before the meat passes from the body it has putrified. The putrification creates gasses which have several ways of causing distress. It also throws toxins off into the body, which leads to various disease conditions.

Therefore it appears it is not the **nature** of man to use meat such as carnivores do. This explanation might seem too crude for your tastes, but this was the way it was explained to me and it seems to agree in principle with other things I've been studying.

And the **Lord** says: wholesome **herbs** are ordained for the **nature** of man. Then it says for the **use** of man. The food we eat must be in a form we can use. I like the little explanation by Dr. Jensen in his book, "Vital Foods for Good Health."[2] He says, "It is not enough to have chemical elements alone. Each food element must carry a life-giving force that will replenish the vital force which our body constantly uses. There is more calcium in the calcimine coating on some walls than in many foods. There would probably be more silicon in a broth made from old shoes than is found in watermelons. Yet there is no question which is the better food."[3] It is a similar case when you need iron. Very often a medical doctor will prescribe ferrous sulfate as an iron supplement. This is a chemical iron which can be quite dangerous to your body.[4] Your body should use only an organic iron. This comes through plants or animals.

So what we eat must be in a form our bodies can **use**. And this should be, for one thing, **all wholesome herbs**.

All wholesome herbs are to be used. We too often get in habits of eating just certain foods and neglect many others which are of equal or even superior quality. In my own case when I heard "vegetable" (notice I use the past tense of the word, because now I have changed!) the word-association would flash a picture in my mind of canned green beans, frozen peas, and corn. Those were the basic vegetables in our meals. Now I see a beautiful full tray of Romaine lettuce, carrot and celery sticks, radishes, cherry tomatoes, cauliflowerettes, and cucumber slices. Or I think of tender steamed asparagus or artichokes; or of the pan of buckwheat lettuce growing in the center of my dining table and the beautiful green wheatgrass to chew on; or the little dishes of delicious mung bean and lentil sprouts to be eaten as finger foods.

This variety of herbs has been the solution to changing my family over to this new way of eating. It's hard enough to change your own habits when you become convinced that such a change is desirable. It's something else to try to change the eating pattern of a family of twelve, especially when several of them are teenagers. I played the same game for starting Day Five that I had used at Day Four when I was trying to introduce my family to foods that were nutritionally superior such as yogurt. I would first tell them how good it was for them and try to get them to eat it. One taste, a screwed-up face, and an "Ugh!" and it was, "No thanks, Mom, I won't eat that stuff." So I would buy enough for myself, find some really delicious way to fix it (such as a yogurt shake made of yogurt, orange juice concentrate, powdered milk, an egg, and whole milk) and sit down and drink it in front of them. They'd turn up their noses and eat their own food. But as time passed one by one the little ones would ask for a taste, smack their lips and say "Mmm!" and ask for some for themselves. Gradually the "middle" aged ones started sampling and finally even a teenager learned to like it. One drawback to this was I had to start buying in larger quantities and even then it was usually gone before I could get any. But this is the way they gradually began to change over.

My husband was worse than the children at Day Four. He just wouldn't eat anything that had a different form or flavor from that which he was used to. When I began my new health plan, (such as having most of the fruits and vegetables raw, no eating starches at the same meal with protein, total abstinence from refined, over-processed foods, etc.) I assumed there was no object in trying to push it off on them. I would simply fix their meal and my meal. They could have macaroni and cheese, green peas and tossed salad. I would have golden baked squash with butter and my personal tray of raw vegetables, very colorful, very crunchy, very delicious. Then they wanted to know if they could have macaroni and cheese and still have the vegetable tray I had. I answered that we could not afford both.

This was the reason we had'nt eaten more raw vegetables before. After buying pancake mix, cake mixes, macaroni, spaghetti, canned soups and canned vegetables and fruits there wasn't enough money to buy fresh produce. We raised our own beef so at least we didn't have that expense.

One or two evenings when I knew the older teenagers would not be home for dinner I would sneak in one of "my" meals on the family. To my surprise my husband accepted this newest program. The food tasted good and although he missed some of our regular food items, I think he felt deep inside this was the right way. Instead of just tolerating my enthusiasm he seemed to be sharing it with me.

Then I got brave and prepared one of these meals when the teenagers were home. They agreed that everything was good, but where was something filling? Unless meat and starch were served at the same meal they felt it wasn't a full meal. My day finally came when my seventeen-year-old son came in hungry from work, sat down at the table and said,

"Hey, that looks great." And I thought it looked "great" too. There was the large crystal lazy susan loaded with crisp, colorful, raw vegetables; two small dishes of salad dressings for dips, and baked fish served on the china platter. The table was set with nice china.

I had made a soup of chicken broth with tiny diced pieces of carrots, celery and green onions cooked till they were just barely tender. With it was served a combination herb tea of nettle, comfrey, red raspberry and red clover.

It was so pretty and the atmosphere was so nice that we took our time eating. With our busy way of life, we're always in such a rush that we don't take time to relax and enjoy our meals. But with raw vegetables to munch it takes longer to eat, and that is better for digestion. And when the meal was over and our appetites were comfortably satisfied, my son said, "Now that was really good."

Chapter VII

IN THE SEASON THEREOF

"Every herb in the season thereof, and every fruit in the season thereof; ..." (D&C 89: 11)

Spring, summer, fall, winter—an eternal round of seasons, at least for those in the temperate zone. And He who created the times and the seasons created the herbs and fruits according to the seasons, providing for man according to his needs.

In the spring there are more fresh fruits and leafy greens necessary for spring cleaning (of our bodies). In the fall the fattening and heat-producing foods are plentiful to prepare our bodies for the cold weather. Consider the fruit which is the main diet of those on the tropical islands. Yet the Eskimo in the far North has a basic diet of meat which creates body heat. Wherever man is found on this earth, the Lord has placed the food which is best suited to his needs.

So why would this simple phrase, "in the season thereof" have been so disturbing to me? It seems to cause a conflict of basic beliefs. On the one hand is the word of the Lord indicating our diet should be based on fresh fruits and vegetables, and on the other hand is our strong reliance on tradition. Tradition in my case dictated a diet based on meat and potatoes with a fruit room stocked with home-canned fruits and vegetables, jams and jellies, pickles and relishes. To "become more perfect" in line with tradition, I had tried to become more proficient in the canning and storing of food. Yet as I pursued this course I was nagged by the question, "Is this in agreement with the phrase 'in the season thereof'?" It is difficult to pursue a course in which you are uncertain. The solution seemed to require that I gain further knowledge in order to have a foundation firm enough to support my belief that what the Lord says is true even if it means breaking with tradition. Tradition can be one of the greatest stumbling blocks as we strive to live the Word of Wisdom more fully. Breaking with tradition is hard even when you have a firm testimony that some other course is better for you.

As I studied and experimented I found many things which confirmed to me the wisdom of the Lord's advice: "in the season thereof." A fruit or vegetable is most nutritious when it is at its peak of ripeness and fresh from the vine or tree. Within a few short hours fruits and vegetables can lose much of their nutritional value. This is one particular reason for growing your own so it can be direct from the garden to the table for full benefit. There are instances where you are better off not to have a particular food at all unless it is locally grown. In the Northwest we cannot grow citrus fruits. In order to get the fruit here fresh it must be picked green. The green citric acid is very harmful to your nerves. Therefore it is better for people here to use another source of Vitamin C. The sprouted mung beans provide 240 milligrams of Vitamin C in each ¼ cup of sprouts. That's equivalent to about five oranges. And the mung sprouts are delicious, tasting like fresh green peas from the pod. In fact, it seems to me that sprouting our grains, beans and seeds is the ideal way to have a continuous supply of fresh greens year around at a nominal cost. The nutritional value of these is increased many times by sprouting, and they become perfect food. (See chapter on sprouting.)

With some of the wild herbs, there is a time when they are in season and are a good source of food, yet when green or too mature they contain certain poisons. So again, the Lord says, "in the season thereof."

We would be foolish and ungrateful if we were to allow the excess to go to waste, so we should preserve the surplus in the manner that will retain the most food value. Frozen food is the next-best thing to fresh food. Food should be picked and into the freezer within an hour or two if at all possible. And it is best to pick it the first thing in the morning when it is the freshest.

Dehydrated foods retain almost all of their nutritional value. It is amazing the multitude of foods you can dry, and they are so delicious for snacks, and when they are reconstituted.

A last resort for preserving is to can. Because of the high heat used to can foods much of the vitamin and enzyme content is destroyed, so this should be used only for foods that cannot otherwise be preserved. You may wonder why, if canned foods are not as good, the church urges us to do home canning. It fits nicely into this Day-One, Day-Two idea. We are always trying to improve on whatever we are doing, and if our food has been mostly packaged or canned from the store, our home-canned foods are a much better value. If you've worked in a cannery and seen the limp, poor quality of some of the produce that is canned you would realize how much better the home-canned product is.

Tomatoes are especially good canned. They can be used in so many ways and should be canned when fully ripe. Use your judgment in these things, with the goal always in mind to upgrade your nutritional program and seek for better health through better habits.

There is a way to have fresh tomatoes off the vine nearly all winter long, and that is to pull the vines which are still loaded with green tomatoes just before the first hard freeze in the fall. Hang them from the rafters in the garage, attic, or other place where it remains cool all the time but does not freeze. The tomatoes will slowly ripen, providing fresh tomatoes for several months. I enjoyed fresh tomatoes from this source in Seattle, Washington, during the last week in February.

Chapter VIII

WITH PRUDENCE
AND THANKSGIVING

Maybe it's because I'm a "skim" reader, or maybe it's because I'm usually in too much of a hurry to take the time to settle down and examine each word or phrase I read, but whatever the reason, whenever I have read the Word of Wisdom I have tended to mentally skip from "in the season thereof" to "yea, flesh also ...," and ignore the statement "all these to be used with prudence and thanksgiving." Perhaps the real reason is that whenever I have read or studied the Word of Wisdom I have been reading for information about health and, if you'll pardon my irreverent attitude, I had the impression that with this statement the Lord had decided to moralize a little. But I was mistaken. When the Lord said "all these things to be used with prudence and thanksgiving" he was still talking about health.

A definition for "prudence" that could be used here would be "cautious practical wisdom." We have already discussed being cautious in our choice of these herbs and fruits, but we should consider another angle. Too much of even a good thing is still too much. Many nutritionists say America's biggest health problem is overeating. 40 million people in America are overweight.

Food is meant (or as the Lord says, ordained) for the use of man—not just to satisfy his appetite. Appetite is one of those things we have to bring under control. The Lord has always condemned gluttony. Therefore, even as we select nutritious foods we should study to see how much our bodies actually require and learn to eat only that amount. Anything over and beyond that is a burden to the body rather than a help.

I was surprised to discover that as the quality of my food increased, the quantity I desired decreased. At one time I would look at a suggested menu of a "healthful" meal and I'd wonder how a person could ever be satisfied with such a meal. It seemed to have no "body" to it. But as I experimented and tried some of these menu ideas, I was delighted at how delicious the meal was and yet my appetite was comfortably satisfied with far less food than I had been used to eating.

"All these to be used with prudence and **thanksgiving**." (D&C 89: 11) Remember as we discussed the Day-One, Day-Two phase I mentioned that at Day Six we would recognize a more comprehensive picture of health, how it not only includes food, air and water, but also includes our mental attitude and our emotional and spiritual attitudes?

In section 88 of the Doctrine and Covenants, just preceding the Word of Wisdom, verse 33 says, "For what doth it profit a man if a gift is bestowed upon him, and he receive not the gift? Behold, he rejoices not in that which is given unto him, neither rejoices in him who is the giver of the gift."

A grateful heart is as important to good health as a nutritional element. Our attitudes drastically affect our health. For example, as you study more about nutrition and see that some of the things you have been eating are not as good for you as others would be, but the things that are good for you don't sound good to you, you grudgingly decide to try them anyway. As you prepare the meal or sit down to eat it you glower at it and gripe, "Well, if this is what I have to eat, I will. But I'll sure not like it." You've failed before you've started! Your attitude will sour your food as surely as vinegar. You may get some improvement in your health over a period of time but that improvement will be greatly impeded by your attitude.

Our thanks should be offered before each meal with sincerity in our hearts for the abundance with which the Lord has blessed us. We should be gratefully aware of the beauty, texture, flavor and nutritional benefits of the foods with which we have been blessed. Even at times when our meals are meager we should consider carefully and perhaps be thankful that we will not have to suffer the consequences of overeating!

In our family we have always called upon someone to offer the "blessing" upon the food. I know of other families who say "grace" before the meal. For the sake of emphasis it might be preferable to call it grace, which to me indicates an attitude of gratefulness rather than asking for a blessing. This might also alleviate another small problem. As the little ones say the blessing, they often include a few phrases generally used in family prayer. It comes out something like this: "Father in Heaven, bless this food. Pray no harm or accident happens to any of us ..." If I didn't realize their sweet innocence I might get the idea they had doubts about my cooking!

Several nutritionists have suggested beginning each meal with prayer as an aid to digestion. To begin a meal with the name of our Heavenly Father and acknowledge His goodness sets a humble, pleasant atmosphere in which to enjoy the meal. Mealtime should always be a pleasant time, a time for quiet, friendly conversation.

Too often mealtime is the only time the whole family is together. Rather than enjoying this togetherness, some fathers use it as a time to reprimand, lecture or lay down the law to the wife and children. Food cannot be properly digested when the stomach is knotted up with fear, humiliation, or resentment.

Another point while we're on attitudes: you might think of the admonition you are given before you partake of the sacrament to the effect that if you are angry with your brother, go to him and make amends first, and then partake of the sacrament. (Matt. 5: 23-24) If you are upset with someone, get it straightened out before you come to the table, or at least put it out of your mind. It is hard on your digestion to eat when you are upset in any way, whether it be anger, pain, or even excessive tiredness.

So healthwise, let prudence guide your appetite and let all your meals be a time of thanksgiving.

Chapter IX

"AND IT IS PLEASING UNTO ME ..."

"Yea, flesh also of beasts and of the fowls of the air, I, the Lord have ordained for the use of man with thanksgiving; nevertheless they are to be used sparingly;

"And it is pleasing unto me that they should not be used, only in times of winter, or of cold, or of famine." (D&C 89: 12-13)

I've pondered much on the words of Elder George A. Smith, delivered in the tabernacle, Great Salt Lake City, March 18, 1855. (J.D. 2: 211-220) The sermon was on the gathering and sanctification of the people of God, but I think it reveals much about the nature of man and his reluctance to obey.

Brother Smith said that from the fall of Adam until the time of Christ, the Lord "could never find a people, could never communicate with a generation or a very numerous body of men that would obey His commandments, listen to His counsel, and observe His wisdom, or be led by His revelations." He said the Lord came close at the time of Enoch, but it was such a small group and the wickedness around was so great that He had to remove Enoch and his city. We know He tried to give the higher law to the people of Moses, but they were unable to receive it so He had to give them a much lesser law. (Inspired Version, Exod. 34: 1-2)

In speaking of the wonderful manifestations and things revealed at the Kirtland temple, Brother Smith said:

"If the Lord had on that occasion revealed one single
sentiment more, or went one step further to reveal more
fully the law of redemption, I believe He would have upset
the whole of us. The fact was, He dare not, on that very
account, reveal to us a single principle further than He had
done, for He had tried, over and over again, to do it. He
tried at Jerusalem; He tried back before the flood; He
tried in the days of Moses, and He had tried, from time to
time, to find a people to whom He could reveal the law of
salvation, and He never could fully accomplish it; and He
was determined this time to be so careful, and advance the
idea so slowly, to communicate them to the children of
men with such great caution that, at all hazards, a few of
them might be able to understand and obey. For, says the
Lord, my ways are not as your ways, nor my thoughts as
your thoughts; for as the heavens are higher than the
earth, so are my ways than your ways, and my thoughts
than your thoughts."

Brother Smith then tells of the persecution the saints
passed through and the sifting and straining from 1837 until
1843—"when the Lord concluded that the people who had
been gathered, since the scattering from Missouri, had been
made acquainted with the principles of His kingdom so long,
that they must have become strong enough for Him to reveal
one sentiment more.

"Wherepon, the Prophet goes up on the stand, and, after
preaching about everything else he could think of in the
world, at last hints at the idea of the law of redemption,
makes a bare hint at the law of sealing, and it produced
such a tremendous excitement that, as soon as he had got
his dinner half eaten, he had to go back to the stand, and
unpreach all that he had preached, and left the people to
guess at the matter."

Has the Lord had to "unpreach" his law of health as it
concerned the eating of meat? If a supposed translation of
an ancient manuscript is true, it would appear He did. There
is a small publication entitled "The Essene Gospel of
Peace" which the translator, Dr. Edmond Bordeaux
Szekely, claims to be translated from a Third-Century
Aramaic manuscript found in the Vatican, which relates the
teachings of Jesus to the Essenes as recorded by John the

Beloved. In this teaching Jesus tells them to eat only live food—foods which best sustain life because they have the germ of life still in them, such as raw fruits and vegetables and grains.

He then tells them that dead food such as meat causes disease and death. This caused quite a stir among these Essene people and they challenged Him with why He was teaching them to abstain from meat and yet Moses taught that only the flesh of unclean animals was forbidden, and they quoted to Him the parts of the Mosaic law referring to eating meat.

Jesus then tells them that when God gave Moses the first tablets of stone containing the laws for His people that He commanded them "Thou shalt not kill" meaning to kill neither man nor beast. But when Moses saw the corruption and weakness of the people he begged the Lord to give them a more lenient law or else surely He would lose all of them for they would never be able to live this higher law. So the Lord watered down the law and said "Thou shalt not kill" would refer to killing man.

Jesus calls to their remembrance what the result of this turned out to be. Not only did they kill the beasts but they continued to kill man also. (The impression I received as I read this was of the Lord throwing up His hands and saying, "What's the use?")

So Jesus seemed to be telling the Essenes, "You asked what you could do to gain health and overcome disease. I've told you plainly. It's up to you now." (**Essene Gospel of Peace** pg. 45-49)

Many times people will point to section 49 of the Doctrine and Covenants, verse 18, to prove that the Lord intends for us to eat meat. Read carefully verses 18 through 21.

"And whoso forbiddeth to abstain from meats, that man should not eat the same, is not ordained of God;

"For, behold, the beasts of the field and the fowls of the air, and that which cometh of the earth, is ordained for the use of man for food and for raiment, and that he might have in abundance.

"But it is not given that one man should possess that which is above another, wherefore the world lieth in sin.

"And wo be unto man that sheddeth blood or that wasteth flesh and hath no need."

It says you should not be **forbidden** to eat meat. Verse 19 says God has ordained the beasts and fowls and things of the earth for the use of man for both food and for raiment, and that in abundance BUT in verse 21 we are cautioned that if we shed their blood and waste the flesh when we have no **need** it's to our condemnation.

If you'll remember, in 1831 when this revelation was given it was not **forbidden** to use tobacco, alcohol, tea and coffee. Many of the saints were using these things. The revelation of section 49 was received in 1831 to counsel a brother, Leman Copley, who had been a Shaker or Shaking Quaker, that he was to preach the doctrines of the true gospel and to be careful to not preach teachings he had carried over from his previous religion. The Word of Wisdom had not yet been given. It was not given for two more years. (Feb. 1833)

Aren't we perhaps like rebellious teenagers who have to be handled with kid gloves? Don't we as parents sometimes allow our teenagers to do things which really aren't for their best good but we allow it rather than have them rebel to the point we would lose them completely?

So as to the eating of meat, the Lord does not require His people to completely abstain from meat at this time. He would be pleased if we ate it sparingly and then only when we really need it such as in the cold or winter or when there is nothing else to eat. And woe to us if we waste it or kill animals for their flesh when we don't really need it.

Obviously if there is nothing else to eat, you would surely eat meat if it were available. Hyrum Smith's explanation of this was that in a famine the animals would die anyway so they shouldn't be left to be wasted but should be eaten. (D&C Commentary, pg. 574) Another point is that the animals eat the grain and grass which could provide food for people so you should eat the animal so it won't eat all the food! I say that with tongue in cheek just to bring out another point. The book, "Diet for a Small Planet" explains that we could get twenty times the protein from the grass and grain the animal eats as we do from eating the animal itself.

As to winter and cold, meat builds heat, so if you are out in the cold a lot and need the extra heat for your body you can get it by eating meat. Even then it should be used sparingly.

We know that in the beginning—in Eden—both man and beast ate herbs or fruit. (P. of G.P., Moses 2: 29-30, 3: 9, 4: 8) In the millennium it will be the same. But it is up to you. Meat is not forbidden. If you choose to eat it then eat it sparingly and then only in time of cold or famine.

If we were to look at meat eating in the light of the "Day-One, Day-Two" system of progress it might go something on this order:

Day One—You eat large quantities of meat with heavy marbled steaks, lots of pork, ham, and bacon.

Day Two—You cut down on the quantity of meat you eat.

Day Three—Give up eating pork (or swine as Brigham Young always called it).

Day Four—You eat meat sparingly, mainly beef and fish.

Day Five—You eat fish and dairy products.

Day Six—You don't even kill fish for food.

Day Seven—Fruits and herbs.

See if there is a connection between this and what Brigham Young was telling the saints in 1868:

"A thorough reformation is needed in regard to our eating and drinking, and on this point I will freely express myself, and shall be glad if the people will hear, believe and obey. If the people were willing to receive the true knowledge from heaven in regard to their diet they would cease eating swine's flesh. I know this as well as Moses knew it, and without putting it in a code of commandments. When I tell you that it is the will of the Lord to cease eating swine's flesh, very likely someone will tell you that it is the will of the Lord to stop eating beef and mutton, and another that it is the will of the Lord to stop eating fowl and fish until the minds of the people become bewildered so that they know not how to decide between right and wrong, truth and error. The beef fed upon our mountain grasses is as healthy food as we need **at present**. (Italics author's.) Beef, so fattened, is as good as wild meat, and is quite different in its nature from stall-fed meat. But we can eat fish, and I ask the people of this community, who hinders you from raising fowls for their eggs? Who hinders you from cultivating fruit of every variety that will flourish in the different parts of this Territory? ... Who hinders any person in this community from having those different kinds of food in their families? Fish is as healthy a food as we can eat, if we except vegetables and fruit, and with them will become a very wholesome diet. What hinders us from surrounding ourselves with an abundance of those various articles of food which will promote health and promote longevity?" (J.D. 12: 192-193)

There are several points in his remarks which we can consider further. He brings out the point that there is a difference between the beef fattened on the mountains and the stall-fed beef. Man seems to always think he can come up with something better than the way the Lord planned things. He has taken up the practice of taking the calves from the cows and feeding them milk supplement, adding things to it to make the calf supposedly disease-free and to produce faster growth. He creates special feed mixtures with added hormones and antibiotics. Although these additives do prevent certain diseases in the animals and do fatten them up quicker, the resultant product is not as good for man as the pasture-raised beef.

Hormones are also given to chickens for rapid growth to make the grower a greater profit, but they have a harmful effect on the person who eats that product.[1] It appears then that whatever meat you eat, it would be better if you raise it yourself, and the Word of Wisdom tells you what feed is best for each animal. (See Ch. 2 of this book)

The counsel to raise our own fish given throughout that period of time (1868) certainly has caught my interest. I'm very eager to dam up a little stream we have on our place and follow the counsel given by the early brethren to raise fish as we do chickens. Physiologists say that fish contain more of the elements necessary to strengthen and build up the brain than almost any other known substance.

So what are we going to eat, and how much, and when, if we honestly want to please the Lord?

Chapter X

THE STAFF OF LIFE

"All grain ... is for the use of man ... to be the staff of life..."

It's odd how ideas get planted in our minds, and once they are planted there and nurtured and used, they assume the status of truth. I had the idea that "staff of life" meant the main stay, the foundation, the main root. Therefore I got the idea that when the Lord said grain was to be the staff of life He meant it was to be the center of our diet, the main item.

So when it was mentioned to me that staff refers to a crutch or a cane I scoffed at the idea. When I looked it up in the dictionary it did indeed have such a definition. With this definition in mind I reread that portion of the Word of Wisdom.

Verse 14:

"All grain is ordained for the use of man and of the beasts to be the staff of life, not only for man but for beasts of the field and the fowls of heaven and all wild animals that run or creep on the earth;

15:

"And these hath God made for the use of man only in times of famine and excess of hunger."

If verse 15 was referring to the grains mentioned in verse 14, then the word "staff" must refer to a crutch or something to lean on when in need. I had been confused about verse 15 because grammatically it seemed to be referring to the grains, but I had always heard that it referred to the animals again, since it had that restrictive clause in it.

We are told to use all wholesome herbs for the constitution, nature, and use of man. Therefore that really is what the basis of our diet should be. Then meat, used sparingly, if at all, in cold or famine. And then grain, as a staff of life, to be used when needed in times of famine or excess hunger. Verse 14 says the grains are to be used by man **and** beast as a staff of life. As a general rule we don't feed animals grain when there is plenty of fresh pasture. It is during the winter when the pasture is low that we feed them grain. This is actually the time **we** need these starchy, heat-producing grains. We should have them stored for times of shortages of the fresh fruits and herbs. In fact, by storing these grains, we assure ourselves of always having fresh herbs on hand! When you have pure, whole grain, you can sprout it and it is then no longer classed as a grain but as an herb. By doing this you increase its nutritional value many times, and it is such a simple thing to do. (See chapter on Sprouting.)

"All grain is good for the food of man; as also the fruit of the vine; that which yieldeth fruit, whether in the ground or above the ground." (D&C 89: 16) We too often get into dull habits, eating the same kinds of foods again and again. The Lord created a vast variety of foods for us, and we should use them. Each one has some element which is helpful to our bodies. If we eat a variety we take advantage of all these nutrients. For instance, cornmeal is very high in magnesium; oatmeal is an excellent source of Vitamin E; rice is high in silicon. These cereal grains may be used whole or cracked as hot breakfast cereals, rolled and very lightly toasted as cold cereal, ground into flour for baking, or used whole in steamed or baked casseroles. As with all foods, they should be the natural whole grain and the less they are cooked, the greater is their nutritional value.

"Nevertheless, wheat for man, and corn for the ox, and oats for the horse, and rye for the fowls and for swine, and for all beasts of the field, and barley for all useful animals, and for mild drinks as also other grain." (D&C 89: 17.)

An interesting story is told as to the wisdom of this statement concerning certain grains for certain animals. A man had two prize-winning oxen. They were very strong and beautiful. He competed in many of the local events, matching his oxen against others. It was suggested by well-meaning friends that he should feed them a certain special grain mixture to keep them in top shape. So he tried it but to his disappointment they lost their sheen and weren't nearly as strong as they had been. You see, he was a mid-western farmer and had grown his own corn, so this was what his oxen had always eaten. The Lord knew "corn for the ox."

It has also been graphically shown that wheat really is the most complete grain for the use of man.[1] An interesting thing about wheat is that when it is sprouted and grows into wheat-grass it is a perfect source of chlorophyll. This chlorophyll has the same atomic structure as the hemoglobin in our blood except that the basic element in chlorophyll is magnesium and in hemoglobin it is iron.[2] Wheat is the most durable grain for storing if it is of the hard winter variety with less than 10% moisture content. Therefore, since grains are to be used as the staff of life, and wheat is the best grain for man, a definite effort should be made to store a good supply of wheat for your family.

As far as rye for fowls, an agriculture department experiment found that when chickens were fed rye their floor droppings were less odorous than when they were fed other grains.!

At least man has been in agreement with the Lord on feeding horses because as far as I've ever seen or heard horses are given oats. Since barley is listed for all useful animals I ran through my mind to see which useful animals were left after the horses, cows, pigs, and chickens were taken care of and I thought of sheep and goats, so evidently they are to eat barley.

Verse 17 says barley is also good for mild drinks, and so are other grains. Pleasant drinks can be made by grinding the grain coarsely and lightly browning it. Then pour hot water over it and let it sit till it cools down, strain, and add a little honey to sweeten. It's not as strong as some of the commercial varieties. Experiment with the different grains to see which you enjoy the most.

With wheat as your main storage item, take stock of what animals you will be feeding and what other grains would add variety to your diet and then store what you need so you will have your staff of life on hand for your use. And then **use** it rather than run to the store for refined, chemicalized, unwholesome flours and cereals.

Chapter XI

REMEMBER—
WALKING IN OBEDIENCE

"And all saints" are to "remember to keep and do these sayings" and be found "walking in obedience to the commandments." (D&C 89: 18)

How well the Lord knows his children! He knows how quick they are to forget. So many times in the scriptures he says to **remember.** Whenever He gives us instructions he reminds us over and over again. He knows that each time He repeats something to us, a few more of us will listen. We will have gained new experiences so we will comprehend more fully because of these experiences. He asks us to remember to keep and do these sayings—these Words of Wisdom.

Some of us have a greater capacity to remember than to **do.** To continue to study and learn all the marvelous facets of proper nutrition and be able to tell others about it comes quite easily for some of us. But the Lord didn't say just to remember them. He said to "keep and do these sayings." Nor are good intentions good enough. The blessings promised in the Word of Wisdom are predicated upon obedience to the law.

My friend, who is so interested in this study, pulled me aside one day and said, "Will you please explain to people that you don't practice all those things you preach. They keep saying if such-and-such is true, how come you have health problems every once in a while too!" It is a point well taken. The truth however is, as I mentioned previously, we will never reach a point of perfect health in this life as it is now. There are too many things going against us. But the biggest thing is still our lack of total obedience to the laws we have been given. And though I study much, and believe much, I still do not **practice** enough! So to us all the Lord says to "remember to keep and **do** these sayings."

And we must not overlook the phrase in verse 18 which says "walking in obedience to the commandments." Our lives are one unified whole. Everything we do in some way affects our health. The Lord says he had never given man a temporal commandment. So though the Word of Wisdom appears to be a temporal commandment because it governs our health, at the same time other very clearly spiritual commandments also affect our health. To gain the promise of the Word of Wisdom requires more than learning to eat the right food. We must be found "walking in obedience to (all) the commandments." Diet, though important, is only a part of the key to good health.

The first and great commandment is to love the Lord. The second is to "love thy neighbor as thyself." Obedience to these commandments is necessary to good health. Perhaps it would be hard to point a finger and say, "Look how healthy he is because he loves." It is possible to illustrate the opposite, however, as we see a person who is physically sick because of hate. Hate, anger, jealousy, covetousness, greed, avarice and lust can poison a person's system as surely as a chemical poison. Also, lacking love for yourself, or losing your self esteem, can drain energy from your body and make you listless, tired, and ill. Emotional problems have physical effects.

In cases of emotional problems such as these, the question might rightly be asked, "Which came first, the chicken or the egg?" Do the emotional problems come first, bringing poor physical health as a result, or does poor physical health lie at the root of the emotional problem? For those who have studied nutrition and understand the extreme results which come from certain nutritional deficiencies, it is heartbreaking to see those poor souls who are confined in mental hospitals and penitentiaries—to realize that a deficiency of some of the B-complex vitamins could very well be responsible for the actions which caused them to be committed. Thiamine (Vitamin B[1]) is a relaxer, an ego builder. A deficiency of this vitamin affects the temperament, causing irritability, low morale, and depression. Pyrodoxine (B[6]) helps keep the nerves young and is a natural tranquilizer. Biotin is considered the mental health vitamin as the lack of it causes mental distress and fatigue. Niacin is the courage vitamin and a lack of it causes feelings of hostility, low morale, tension and jealousy.[1]

These B-complex vitamins which are so important to our emotional well-being are almost totally destroyed in our common refined foods.[2] How much more effective would the therapy and rehabilitation of these people be if they could receive adequate (or, better yet, **under proper supervision,** massive amounts) of these essential vitamins.[3] And how much easier would it be for all of us to "walk in obedience." if we received the optimum amounts of these important nutrients which give us the natural desire to do right.

Another commandment which, if obeyed, would have an important effect upon our health is "Remember the sabbath day to keep it holy." Even the Lord rested on the seventh day. He knew it was necessary and He has given us the commandment to do likewise. Yet many of us allow our desire for money to keep us on the job seven days a week. Others use Sunday as a holiday for games and play rather than a holy day of rest. Others put in many long hours on Sunday doing church work, some of which could perhaps be done at another time through better planning. The purpose of the sabbath day is to build spirituality but to allow the mind and body to rest. (See Brigham Young's ideas on this. J.D. 8:57-58)

Besides observing the **day** of rest, we should use better judgment in our daily work. The old saying, "a man works from sun to sun but a woman's work is never done" is a true saying; so use reason: if a woman's work is never done, why try to do it all in one day? Brigham Young advised, "Instead of doing two days' work in one day, wisdom would dictate to our sisters, and to every other person, that if they desire long life and good health, they must, after sufficient exertion, allow the body to rest before it is entirely exhausted." (J.D. 12: 122)

In the Doctrine and Covenants, 88: 124, the Lord tells us to "cease to sleep longer than is needful; retire to thy bed early, that ye may not be weary; arise early, that your bodies and your minds may be invigorated." At one time man followed these two practices—of working from sun to sun and of arising early and retiring early. Man lived by the sun. The Lord gave us the sun to light the day for us to do our work and the night to allow us to rest. But then came the light bulb, TV and radio, and now we're all mixed up.

Besides these direct physical effects from obeying or disobeying the commandments, there is another very important reason that walking in obedience affects our health. As one studies the gospel he comes to understand that each time we obey a commandment we draw closer to our Heavenly Father and we are more worthy of having His Spirit to dwell with us. Each time we disobey, we are putting ourselves further into Satan's realm of influence. Therefore obedience to the other commandments puts us in a position to more easily obey the Word of Wisdom. On the other hand, if we are not keeping the other commandments, Satan has a much greater influence to make us succumb to the temptations of breaking the Word of Wisdom also.

So remember: keep and do these sayings and walk in obedience to all the commandments the Lord has given us and you will be worthy to receive the promised blessings.

Chapter XII

HEALTH TO THE NAVEL, MARROW TO THE BONE

Have you ever read the Old Testament version of the Word of Wisdom? "My son, forget not my law; but let thine heart keep my commandments; For length of days, and long life, and peace, shall they add to thee.

"Let not mercy and truth forsake thee: bind them about thy neck; write them upon the table of thine heart: So shalt thou find favour and good understanding in the sight of God and man.

"Trust in the Lord with all thine heart; and lean not unto thine own understanding. In all thy ways acknowledge him, and He shall direct thy paths.

"Be not wise in thine own eyes: fear the Lord, and depart from evil. It shall be health to thy navel, and marrow to thy bones." (Prov. 3: 1-8)

Health to the navel and marrow in the bones seems to be the capstone of good health. These were elusive phrases to me for a long time. I'm not sure I have a full understanding of their import even yet but there are two vital factors here that I can comprehend to a degree. To be "born of goodly parents" as was Nephi is a great blessing. (1 Nephi 1: 1) If at the time of conception, the mother is in good health, she conveys to her unborn child health and strength which the child receives through the cord of life, its navel. Therefore "health in the navel" would indicate a blessing not only for yourself but for your posterity. We know that the sins of the parents are visited upon the children to the third and fourth

generations. (Mosiah 13:13) The birth defects in children
are often the result of poor nutrition on the part of the
mother, which causes the child to be deficient in some of the
essential elements necessary for proper formation and
growth.

Studies the past few years have shown the high
incidence of deformities of the hearts of babies born to
parents who drink alcohol. These deformities, which
include a hole or holes in the heart, or even situations where
the heart develops outside the chest cavity, can be caused by
alcoholic consumption by either the father or the mother,
and the chances of deformity are greatly increased if either
or both are alcoholics. Another study has shown that there
were birth defects in 71% of the babies born to women who
drink alcohol. But the rest of the report was just as startling:
there are 35% born with defects even when the parents don't
drink, which points up the fact that there are problems other
than drinking, and many of these are because of the
inadequate diet of the mothers.

Dr. Lendon Smith, M.D., a noted pediatrician, explains
another reason why nutrition during and previous to
pregnancy is so vital. He sites as an example certain cases
of homosexuality. He states that each child is conceived
with a female brain. Sometime during the first few months
of the pregnancy, if it is a male child, the hormone androgen
wafts over the baby's brain. This programs the brain for
masculinity. If for some reason this hormone does not
perform at that point in development, the brain remains
with feminine tendencies. Then when the boy reaches the
age of 13 the hormone testostrone is released and charges
sex activity within the young man. Unfortunately the
emotional portion of his brain is still feminine and thus he
becomes sexually attracted to males rather than females, a
handicap he will find difficult to overcome. Though there
are also other causes for such unnatural tendencies, some
nutritional, some emotional and some social, nevertheless
no mother or mother-to-be would want to be responsible for
such a situation to result from her own inadequate diet.

It would appear that there is a tremendous responsibility on us to live so that we are worthy to receive the promised blessing of health to the navel, especially for the sake of our children.

Our blood is made in the marrow of the bone. Blood is the life element in our bodies. It is the transportation system which carries all the nutrients and oxygen to all the cells in our bodies. A healthy body depends on healthy blood. Diseases known to be associated with the lack of healthy marrow in the bone include leukemia and Hodgkin's disease. The promise of "marrow to the bone" may be of even greater significance than we realize at this time. This promise is granted upon obedience to the Lord's law of health. We must learn to live the Lord's way rather than by our own wisdom. The Word of Wisdom is a stepping stone to lead us to the Lord's way.

Chapter XIII

TREASURES OF KNOWLEDGE

"And shall find wisdom and great treasures of knowledge, even hidden treasures ..." (D&C 89: 19)

Herophilus said, "When health is absent wisdom cannot reveal itself or it cannot manifest, strength cannot fight, wealth becomes useless, and intelligence cannot be applied."

Were a person to obey the Word of Wisdom and yet for one reason or another not gain total health, it would still be worth all the effort put forth if he gained this promise of wisdom and knowledge. This is perhaps the greatest part of the Word of Wisdom promise.

One of the most miraculous gifts we have from God is our brain with its vast capacity for learning, directing and recording. No computer yet designed comes anywhere near having the capacity and ability of the human mind. It has been said that in his lifetime man does not use even one-tenth of his brain's potentiality. If we were to properly care for our health, we could greatly increase our mental powers by allowing our brains to function more efficiently. At one time a doctor told me I was anemic in the head! (It sounded like a taunt my children might use!) But his view was that many, if not most, people had this condition because the oxygen was not getting to the brain in sufficient quantities to accomplish its purpose. The cell tissue cannot fully function without oxygen, and oxygen is carried to the cells by the blood. If the blood's circulation is not good, the brain is one of the areas to suffer the most. Some of the things we can do to help overcome this brain "anemia" is to have proper nutrition, do slant-board exercises (this helps get the blood up into the head better), sleep with our heads to the north (the magnetic pull on the iron in the blood brings it into the brain area[1]) and work for good blood circulation to the feet. (If the blood circulation is poor in the feet it is poor in the head.[2])

Besides the physical stimulation for the brain we must actively stimulate it mentally. It should be quite obvious that when the Lord promises us wisdom and great treasures of knowledge, even hidden treasures, He wasn't going to just shower this down upon our heads. He has promised that when we **seek** then we shall find; that we are to read and study, and teach one another. If we diligently study to learn the mind and will of God, and then apply that which we learn, He opens up new avenues for us to investigate. In all things we learn by "line upon line, precept upon precept; here a little, and there a little." (D&C 128:21)

George Q. Cannon said, "It is true, probably, that there are many points concerning our welfare that may not have been touched upon by our Heavenly Father in the Word of Wisdom, but in my experience I have noticed that they who practice what the Lord has alread given us are keenly alive to other words of wisdom and counsel that may be given .... There are a thousand ways in which we can act unwisely; our attention has been directed to some few points, and if we observe them the Lord has promised us great treasures of wisdom, which will enable us to see a thousand points where we can take better care of our bodies, preserve our health, and which will enable us to train our children in the way of the Lord. The results will be that our children will be healthy and strong, and we will raise up a generation that will be a blessing to us, and through whom the Lord can accomplish His great and mighty works in the earth." (J.D. 12:44-45)

Chapter XIV

RUN AND NOT BE WEARY

The promise continues "And shall run and not be weary, and shall walk and not faint." (D&C 89:20) As we apply correct rules of health in our diet, we notice a definite effect upon our ability to work and play. We find that our desire to get up and get at it is greatly increased, our endurance is greater, and a greater sense of achievement comes to us as we are able to more efficiently fulfill our desires and responsibilities.

But if we stop at diet and don't improve in other health habits we are going to miss part of the blessings we could otherwise enjoy. Assuming that we have improved our diet and have noticed the difference it has made, what would be the next logical step in order to fully achieve the promise of being able to run and not be weary and walk and not faint? Obviously it would be to do a little running or a little walking and see how it goes. To assume that the improvement of diet would make it possible for you to take off on a fifty-mile hike and smile to the end is a little ridiculous. Ask your Boy Scout son or neighbor how he gets prepared for his fifty miler. In all probability he will tell you of the several five- and ten-mile hikes he had to take first to get in shape.

So it is with us. If we want to run and not be weary then we had better start doing a little jogging every morning or evening and get our muscles toned up a bit. Over-enthusiasm in this can be disastrous. Overdo it the first time or two and you'll be kneading cramped muscles well into the wee hours of the morning. Take it easy. Start slowly and gradually build up and then try to be consistent. Consistent exercise is an excellent way to build self-discipline.

Maybe jogging isn't your thing. There are some authorities on the subject who feel that walking is even more beneficial than jogging.[1] They suggest that you set a definite stride and make it a purposeful thing, not just meandering along. Whatever you decide to do, whether it is jogging, walking, swimming, calisthenics, or whatever, be consistent. Constantly strive to improve and you will see in a very short time how much longer and faster you can run without tiring and how much greater is your endurance in walking.

Exercise is the best possible remedy for fatigue. Brigham Young counseled that when your mind becomes tired, go and exercise you body. (J.D. 6: 148) Some doctors recommend that when women get that mid-morning letdown, that's a good time to stop and do their exercises. The slantboard exercises[2] are especially good at times like that because they cause the blood circulation to increase to the head, which in turn gets the oxygen there to help wipe out those cobwebs. At the same time you are in a position to let your body rest and relax.

Another way to look at the idea of "run and not be weary and walk and not faint" is given by Amasa Lyman in 1855. "Do not work yourselves to death, but try to live a long time, and learn to run and not weary, walk and not faint. Do you think leaving off tea and coffee, alone, will enable you to scale mountains, and outstrip the mountain goat in fleetness? It is just as true that weariness is the consequence of excessive toil as that God lives and reigns. It is manifest in you and me, and in every other part of His work. Keep the Word of Wisdom; and if you want to run and not weary, walk and not faint, call upon me and I will tell you how—just stop before you get tired." (J.D. 3: 176)

Chapter XV

THE DESTROYING ANGEL

"And I, the Lord, give unto them a promise, that the destroying angel shall pass by them, as the children of Israel, and not slay them." (D&C 89:21)

When the Lord was bringing the several plagues against Egypt in order to make Pharaoh let the children of Israel go out from bondage, His final condition was that unless Pharaoh let them go, He would slay the first-born of all the Egyptians. In order for this "destroying angel" to pass by the children of Israel they were to slay an unblemished lamb and spread its blood on the door posts of each Hebrew home. At the sight of that sign the destroying angel would pass over that house and not slay anyone in it. History records that because of his intense grief over the loss of his own only son, Pharaoh did let them go, and since that time the Hebrews have celebrated the Feast of the Passover in gratitude to the Lord for their deliverance.

Several times the Lord has compared modern Israel (The Church of Jesus Christ of Latter-day Saints) with ancient Israel. He alluded to Joseph Smith receiving commandments and revelations as did Moses (D&C 28:2) He compared the exodus of the saints from Nauvoo, led by Brigham Young, to the exodus from Egypt led by Moses. And now in the closing words of the Word of Wisdom He promises the saints that if they obey the Word of Wisdom "the destroying angel will pass by them as the children of Israel and not slay them."

It appears there is one main difference between the two situations. The Hebrews went out on the appointed night and slew the lambs and painted the door posts with the blood. It was the **sign** that was necessary for the destroying angel to pass by. It seems very doubtful that there will be an appointed night or day in which the saints can suddenly obey the Word of Wisdom and the destroying angel will pass by. The Word of Wisdom seems to be a law which offers protection in direct proportion to the degree of obedience. Neither does it seem probable that the destroying angel of the last days is to have a one-night errand of destruction. In the Doctrine and Covenants, section 86, verse 5, we are told, "Behold, verily I say unto you, the angels are crying unto the Lord day and night, who are ready and waiting to be sent forth to reap down the fields ..." That was in December, 1832.

Now hear the words of Wilford Woodruff spoken in 1894 as recorded in the Millennial Star:

> "What is the matter with the world today? What has created this change that we see coming over the world? Why these terrible earthquakes, tornados and judgments? What is the meaning of all these mighty events that are taking place? The meaning is, these angels that have been held for many years in the temple of our God have got their liberty to go out and commence their mission and their work in the earth, and they are here today in the earth."[1]

It is true that earthquakes and other natural disasters continue to increase in the earth today. But it isn't very evident how obedience to the Word of Wisdom could give us protection from this type of destruction. There are possibly other manifestations of the destroying angel present in the world today, however, from which we can and should protect ourselves through obedience to the Word of Wisdom.

Statistics on causes of death are compiled and reviewed and revised constantly. Although science claims to have stopped some of the great killers of the ages, yet other diseases take their place and increase daily in their toll of lives.

Some of the more prevalent killers of today's "civilized" world are cancer, cardiovascular diseases, and respiratory diseases. It is now common knowledge that living by the very basic Word of Wisdom, that is, not using tea, coffee, alcohol, and tobacco, is among the best measures people can take to protect themselves from these dread diseases. Yet even people who do not use these substances are sometimes afflicted with these particular diseases, showing that there are other causes of these diseases and therefore other protective measures necessary. Living the fuller law of the Word of Wisdom would increase one's protective powers over these diseases.

Diabetis, cancer and arthritis can be brought on by improper diet and in many instances have been cured through proper diet. I realize this is a controversial statement, but I believe there is enough evidence to substantiate it. It is frightening what influence "evil and designing men" have over the minds of the people in these latter days. Truths which could alleviate much pain and suffering and avoid untimely death are kept from the people or discredited by "authorities" or "experts."[2]

There are, however, many doctors and researchers who have published works to inform people of the natural ways to overcome sickness and disease. **The Cancer News Journal**[3] is a bi-monthly publication which presents the views of spokesmen for a variety of non-toxic therapies for cancer. Reading an interview with Dr. William Donald Kelley in the January-February 1973 issue, I was struck by his definition of cancer. He claims, "Cancer ... is the inability of the body to properly metabolize protein—just as diabetis is the inability of the body to metabolize carbohydrates and sugars."

It is interesting to observe in Dr. Kelley's therapy that he recommends using nuts and vegetable proteins, which are more easily digested than the meat proteins. After four or five months on his program a patient can add soft-boiled egg, yogurt and fish to his diet. But the meat proteins seem to be the proteins that cause problems of digestion and metabolism, thus becoming the cancer-causing agent.

The book and filmstrip "World Without Cancer" by G. Edward Griffin, explains how cancer is a chronic, metabolic disease and shows the benefits of proper and specific nutrition in its prevention and cure.

Using too many sweets and refined food products seems to be a contributing factor in the incidence of diabetis. The refining process removes many of the B vitamins which are essential for the proper use of carbohydrates by the body. Because diabetis precipitates so many other problems in the body, a person should use a preventive diet so diabetis never gets a start. Prevention is far, far easier than correction.

A book by Giraud W. Campbell, D.O.,[4] tells of amazing arthritis cures in **seven days**! This seven-day program is used for both osteoarthritis and rheumatoid arthritis. It consists of one day of fasting, followed by a total natural **raw food diet** with no refined, preserved foods at all. Later, vitamin and mineral supplements are added. This simple program has brought total relief from pain and stiffness in as little as one week. It not only brings relief from the pain and stiffness of the disease but can actually repair the damage to bones and joints. Dr. Campbell says: "The cause of the weakening of the bones and joints is due to wrong diet." He shows before-and-after X-rays of hip joints, knee joints and spinal deterioration revealing repair of the arthritic damage which has occurred within six to eight months of strictly adhering to right diet. You will need to read his book to learn exactly how to use his programs.

Rather than trying to go into other of the many diseases and steps which could be taken to improve each specific condition, the next chapters will dwell on two other possible manifestations of the destroying angel.

Chapter XVI

IS THE DESTROYING ANGEL IATROGENIC DISEASES?

The term iatrogenic disease means doctor-drug caused disease.

Diagnosis appears to be the biggest problem in the field of medicine. Statistics have shown that the Mayo Brothers' Clinic has been, in the past, only 42 percent correct in their diagnoses.[1] Considering the advanced technical equipment of the Mayo Brothers and their vast experience, one would have to assume that a regular medical doctor's diagnostic successes would be much less. Since doctors treat according to their diagnoses, obviously their rate of "cures" could not exceed this same percentage.

One doctor, on looking back on his medical career, remarked that of the 5000 appendectomies he had performed, probably only two were really necessary.[2]

Brigham Young had quite strong feelings about doctors and doctoring. He said:

> I say that unless a man or woman who administers medicine to assist the human system to overcome disease, understands and has that intuitive knowledge, by the Spirit, that such an article is good for that individual at that very time, they had better let him alone. Let the sick do without eating, take a little of something to cleanse the stomach, bowels and blood, and wait patiently, and let Nature have time to gain the advantage over the disease." (J.D. 15: 225)

Joseph Smith also had a word to say about medicine:

"I preached to a large congregation at the stand, on the science and practice of medicine, desiring to persuade the Saints to trust in God when sick, and not in the arm of flesh, and live by faith and not by medicine, or poison; and when they are sick, and had called for the elders to pray for them, and they were not healed, to use herbs and mild food." (DHC VI: 414)

If you notice, neither of these prophets suggests that you ignore the problem or just sit by and see; they gave specific steps to take instead of calling a doctor.

I have always been very tolerant of my doctors in the way they handle the problems of my children and myself because (1) it was my own fear or lack of knowledge or confidence that sent me to them in the first place and (2) I realize that during all their years of training and study they receive only a minute portion of nutritional studies, and these are geared mainly to learning of certain dangers from "overdose" of particular vitamins. Their training is not toward preserving or maintaining superior health but rather toward treating problems or bringing relief from symptoms.[3] Theirs is a study of medicine and surgery.

Tolerant or not, I found it very discouraging to go to a doctor and be told that the problem I had was "normal." When my boys reached the age of ten or twelve they each had periods of leg cramps. Upon consulting the doctor, at the child's request, we were told this is "normal" for boys that age. These are sometimes referred to as growing pains for lack of a scientific name, and the child will outgrow them. Well, so they did, but with frequent discomfort. With a little more study of nutrition I learned that because of the rapid growth at this stage, there is a calcium deficiency. With supplements of natural calcium (calcium lactate from milk or organic calcium from plants) these leg cramps were quickly relieved when my younger boys reached that age.

One evening the blood vessels on my hands became very distended, my ankles were swollen, I had a rash on most of my body, a very rapid heart beat and respiration, and I was very weak. Almost in panic I phoned the doctor and described my situation. He told me to go immediately to his office, where he would meet me. Upon my arrival he took one look at me and said, "Oh, I didn't realize you were pregnant. This is quite normal with pregnancy." (This was my eighth pregnancy and I had never had this "normal" reaction before.)

I consider myself lucky because my doctors seldom did anything for these conditions. Of course they are aware of my aversion to drugs. Often a doctor will write a prescription or give a shot just to satisfy a patient, and often at the insistence of the patient. It is in this area of doctoring that trouble can begin. Each year a doctor receives a large book listing all the new drugs, their uses, and their side effects. Although sometimes these drugs do help, often the side effects from them are worse than the original problem. It is reported that "1,120,000 persons are admitted to hospitals each year because of drug-induced illness—over 5,000,000 hospital patients annually suffer one or more episodes of medical complications. It is estimated that drugs and medical therapy kill, or contribute, to the death of 100,000 Americans each year!"[4]

Hippocrates, who is credited with being the Father of Medicine, said a doctor should never administer a poison to a person—that he should use only medicinal herbs. Yet today's medical profession uses such "medicines" as strychnine, arsenic and nitro-glycerin as well as the thousands of non-herbal drugs. Dr. Henry E. Simmons of the F.D.A. reported that excessive use of antibiotics may be killing upwards of 30,000 people a year, and studies show that about 60 percent of all hospitalized patients are given the drugs even when they don't show any signs of infection.[5]

To protect ourselves from such a weapon of the destroying angel requires study, faith, and prayer. Diligent adherence to the Word of Wisdom will make running to the doctor a thing of the past except, as Brigham Young said, when we need a bone set or emergency surgery. (JD 15: 225) At such times we should let the doctors know that we want as little medication as possible.

Chapter XVII

COULD THE DESTROYING ANGEL BE ENVIRONMENTAL DISEASE?

A second possible manifestation of the destroying angel is much more insidious. It is something that is increasing in huge proportions daily. This is known as Environmental Disease.[1] This threat, which is world-wide, results from pollution. We hear much about the air pollution from automobile exhaust, industrial emissions, raw sewage and detergents released in our waterways and the dangerous freon gas used in aerosol spray cans. All of these are a definite threat to our health and the health of all earth life. Yet the most insidious of all pollution threats to health is radiation. The greatest cause of hazardous radiation comes from fallout or ground seepage from nuclear-bomb detonation and testing. Next in line, in spite of violent denials to the contrary, are nuclear power plants. And, in our daily "civilized" activities we encounter a third major source of radiation—our modern (and some not so modern) inventions such as X-ray machines, color TV, micro-wave ovens and towers, the laser beam, food irradiation, luminous watch and clock dials, and fluorescent lights, just to name a few.[2]

The frightening danger from nuclear tests is that thousands of tons of radioactive material are sucked into the air. Some of this falls immediately to earth. Some is picked up by winds and swept around the world, gradually spilling down in rain or snow. Some particles rise as high as the stratosphere and may take from one to ten years to sift down. Add to this the fact that there is a characteristic five-year delay in the onset of disease following exposure to children or pregnant mothers, and you see a force threatening not only immediate reactions but a potentially more dangerous future destruction.[3]

What are some of the effects of this radiation pollution? "Anemia, boring pains in the bones, and other bone disorders, cyctic conditions, warts which become sore or swollen, recurring attacks of flu, gastroenteritis, headaches, tiredness which no amount of rest can relieve, numb hands and feet, boils, carbuncles, skin rashes, breathlessness, weakness, confused and mental states with inability to remember, parched skin, a type of weeping sinus trouble, inflamed roof of mouth with swelling, buzzing in the ears, loss of appetite, distended or bloated abdomen, constipation, insomnia, dimming vision and falling hair" are symptoms an Australian doctor found traceable to radioactive fallout.

Other effects listed by other doctors are leukemia, cancer, sterility, cataracts, epilepsy, paraplegia, ulcers, genetic damage.

As is very evident, most of these are what we consider common ailments. The evidence which points to a radioactivity-cause-connection is that as the recorded radiation level rises there is a sharp increase in severity or deaths from these diseases.[4]

Although it is the responsibility of each of us to study and do all we personally can to prevent further pollution of our environment, and thus strive to protect not only our own health but also the health and lives of future generations, the work of "evil and designing men" and many others who are simply misguided, continues to increase these dangers in our lives. Rather than leave us at the mercy of these destructive forces, the Lord has given us the promise that if we obey the Word of Wisdom the destroying angel will pass by us and not slay us.

To understand how this can be, we must understand the nature of radioactive fallout and some of the other forms of radiation pollution. The radioactive particles do not actually contaminate the body. "They merely absorb the minerals, the protective elements, from the bones and blood, thus leaving the body more or less powerless to carry on the normal functions such as digestion, assimilation, elimination of waste matter, and the reproduction of new cells."[5]

So as we pursue our study of the Word of Wisdom and nutrition we learn how to fortify and refortify our bodies with elements which are being destroyed by this radiation. Some specific foods have been found to be especially effective in protecting the body against radioactivity. Pectin proves to be helpful as it seems to attract, bind and eliminate radiation from the system. It can be found in apples, lemons and sunflower seeds. Sprouted seeds such as buckwheat, wheat, mung or soy beans, and alfalfa, seem to be effective protection also. Minerals seem to be a key factor in protection against radiation so any source especially rich in minerals should be considered.

We should use care in the selection and handling of our foods so we do not add more radiation to our bodies through the foods we eat. Leafy greens resist fallout, as do smooth vegetables and fruits. Washing all your fruits and vegetables with a biodegradable cleaning product or with a little cider vinegar in water will help remove about 60 percent of the surface radiation. Nut meats are protected by the nut shells so they are a good source of protein.

In summary: following all the best rules of nutrition, avoiding worthless foods and adding those foods which are most nutritious is the best protection you can give yourself from the destroying angel, assuming you are at the same time striving to walk in obedience to the other commandments of God.

Chapter XVIII

THE KEY TO
HEALTH AND LONGEVITY

Brigham Young said if we would only learn to obey we could look forward to a happy, useful lifetime of hundreds of years rather than becoming decrepit and going to the grave at seventy.

"We can enjoy the blessings of heaven, or we can deprive ourselves of that enjoyment. Intelligent beings have the power to exercise their free will and choice in doing good, equally as much as in doing evil. All have the privilege of doing evil if they are disposed so to do, but they will always find that the wages of sin is death. The Latter-day Saints, by their righteousness, can enjoy all the blessings which the Lord has promised to bestow upon His people, and they can, by their unrighteousness, deprive themselves of the enjoyment of those blessings. We, for instance, exhort the Saints to observe the Word of Wisdom, that they may, through its observance, enjoy the promised blessing. Many try to excuse themselves because tea and coffee are not mentioned, arguing that it refers to hot drinks only. What did we drink hot when that Word of Wisdom was given? Tea and coffee. It definitely refers to that which we drink with our food. I said to the Saints at our last annual Conference, the Spirit whispers to me to call upon the Latter-day Saints to observe the Word of Wisdom, to let tea, coffee, and tobacco alone, and to abstain from drinking spiritouous drinks. This is what the Spirit signifies through me. If the Spirit of God whispers this to His people through their leader, and they will not listen nor obey, what will be the consequence of their disobedience? Darkness and blindness of mind with regard to the things of God will be their lot; they will cease to have the spirit of prayer, and the spirit of the world will increase in them in proportion to their disobedience until they apostatize entirely from God and His ways.

"This is no new or strange thing that you are required to do. Thirty-five years ago we were called upon to reform in our lives, by giving heed to the same Words of Wisdom; and if any man comes to you and tells you that you must have a little tea and a little coffee, by the same rule he may urge you to take a little tobacco and a little intoxicating liquor, or a little of any other substance which is hurtful to man. This destroys their claim and right to the spirit of revelation, and they go into darkness. There is not a single Saint deprived of the privilege of asking the Father, in the name of Jesus Christ, our Savior, if it is true that the Spirit of the Almighty whispers through His servant Brigham to urge upon the Latter-day Saints to observe the Word of Wisdom. All have this privilege from the apostle to the lay member. Ask for yourselves.

"...Why should we continue to practise in our lives those pernicious habits that have already sapped the foundation of the human constitution, and shortened the life of man to that degree that a generation passes away in the brief period of from twenty-seven to twenty-nine years? The strength, power, beauty and glory that once adorned the form and constitution of man have vanished away before the blighting influences of inordinate appetite and love of this world. Doubtless we are about the best-looking people today upon this footstool, and about the healthiest; but where is the iron constitution, the marrow in the bone, the power in the loins, and the strength in the sinew and muscle of which the ancient fathers could boast? These have, in great measure, passed away; they have decayed from generation to generation, until constitutional weakness and effeminacy are bequeathed to us through the irregularities and sins of our fathers. The health and power and beauty that once adorned the noble form of man must again be restored to our race; and God designs that we shall engage in this great work of restoration. Then let us not trifle with our mission, by indulging in the use of injurious substances. These lay the foundation of disease and death in the systems of men, and the same are committed to their children, and another generation of feeble human beings is introduced into the world. Such children have insufficient bone, sinew, muscle, and constitution, and are of little use to themselves, or to their fellow creatures; they are not prepared for life, but for the grave; not to live five, six, eight, and nine hundred years, but to appear for a moment, as it were, and pass away. Now, when a person is fifty years of age he or she is considered an old man or an old woman; they begin to feel decrepit, and think they must feel old, appear old, and begin to die. Premature death is in the marrow of their bones, the seeds of early dissolution are sown in their bodies, they feel old at fifty, sixty, and seventy years, when they should feel like boys of fifteen, sixteen, and seventeen. Instead of feeling decrepit at those years they should feel full of strength, vigor, and life, having attained to early maturity, prepared now to enter upon the duties of a long future life, and when two hundred years have been attained, they should then feel more vigorous than the healthiest of men do in this age at forty and fifty years." (J.D. 12:117-119)

What was the key to health that gave Adam 936 years of life, Enos 905 years, Methuselah 969 years and Noah 650? Obviously it is to avoid those "pernicious habits" of tea, coffee, tobacco, alcohol and drugs. There is also the possibility it has something to do with eating "live" food. Another term for live foods as found in the record of the Essenes is "eating from the table of God." It is recorded thus:

"So eat always from the table of God: the fruits of the trees, the grains and grasses of the fields, the milk of beasts, and the honey of bees. For everything beyond these is of Satan, and leads by the way of sins and diseases unto death. But the foods which you eat from the abundant table of God give strength and youth to your body, and you will never see disease. For the table of God fed Methuselah of old, and I tell you truly, if you live even as he lived, then will the God of the living give you also long life upon the earth as was his." (Essene Gospel, pg. 51)

If "live food" equals life and "dead food" equals death (ibid pg. 49) it's a miracle we live as long as we do, considering the amount of dead food we eat in comparison to the amount of live food.

We bake our bread—dead.

We kill our meat and eat it—dead.

We cook our fruits and vegetables—dead.

What is meant by "live food"? If you pick fruits and vegetables, doesn't that kill them dead the same as when you kill an animal? No. Once you kill an animal it cannot grow again or reproduce itself. But pull up a carrot, break off the top, cut the carrot off about one-fourth inch from the top. Put that little cap in a jar lid with water covering the bottom. In a few days a fresh green top will start to grow. (Which, by the way, is very good to eat.) A cherry pit will start a new tree; a potato can be planted and start a new potato plant. Therefore fruits and vegetables retain life within themselves UNTIL you cook them. When you cook them at a temperature above 150 degrees you kill them; that is, you destroy the life element within them. A roasted nut, a cooked prune, a baked potato, cannot reproduce. Seed grains can be stored in dry places for hundreds of years and still grow when they are planted, but not if you bake them.

So how is it we live as long as we do? Purely as a matter of speculation, let's consider that perhaps one-tenth of the food we eat is "live" food. Let's assume that from Adam till Noah, most of the righteous people of God were eating 95 percent live food. Today we look forward to a life of 70 years or, in some cases, 95 years or above. The patriarchs of the Old Testament had life spans of 600 to 969 years. Is there a possible connection?

10% live food—100 years?

95% live food—950 years?

As mentioned before, in the Garden of Eden, Adam ate fruit. (Moses 4: 8) What did the Lord tell him to eat when he was cast out of the Garden? "And thou shalt eat the herb of the field." (Moses 4: 34) Then we are told that "Adam began to till the earth, and to have dominion over all the beasts of the field, and to eat his bread by the sweat of his brow ..." (Moses 5: 1) It does not say he ate the beasts—it says he had dominion over them. He used their wool, their milk; used them to carry him, perhaps to help him till the soil.

But compare this to the instructions He gave to Noah following the flood. "Be fruitful and multiply, and replenish the earth. And **the fear of you** and the dread of you shall be upon every beast of the earth, and upon every fowl of the air, upon all that moveth upon the earth, and upon all the fishes of the sea; into your hand are they delivered.

"Every moving thing that liveth shall be meat for you; **even as the green herb** have I given you all things.

"But the blood of all flesh which I have given you for meat, shall be shed upon the ground, which taketh life thereof, and the blood ye shall not eat.

And surely, blood shall not be shed, only for meat, **to save your lives;** and the blood of every beast will I require at your hands." (Inspired Version, Gen. 9: 8-11)

This seems to bear out the fact that herbs had been the approved food up until that time. What the reason was for giving Noah this instruction to eat meat we are not told except it appears that because of the flood there was a scarcity of food. So Noah was told that they could eat meat to save their lives. There may have been other changes occurring at the time of the flood which caused the life span of man to be shortened. Perhaps when he started eating meat he started cooking over a fire and decided to cook his fruit and herbs too!

This fear which came upon the beasts at that time will be taken from them in the millennium. Isaiah tells us, "The wolf also shall dwell with the lamb, and the leopard shall lie down with the kid; and the calf and the young lion and the fatling together; and a little child shall lead them.

"And the cow and the bear shall feed; their young ones shall lie down together: and the lion shall eat straw like the ox.

"And the suckling child shall play on the hole of the asp, and the weaned child shall put his hand on the cockatrice's den.

"They shall not hurt nor destroy in all my holy mountain; for the earth shall be full of the knowledge of the Lord, as the waters cover the sea." (Isaiah 11: 6-9)

And in that day we are told the child will live to be a hundred years old and a man's life shall be the age of a tree. (D&C 101:30; Isaiah 65:20,22)

To live to be a hundred or hundreds of years old would be terrible if such years were to be filled with the pain and suffering of disease. But living the Word of Wisdom promises us a full, rich, happy life where all our faculties are fully productive.

The pattern of eating food appears to be thus:

Garden of Eden	- fruit
Adam to Noah	- fruit and herbs
Noah to Us	- fruit, herbs, meat
? ? ?	- fruit and herbs
Millennium	- fruit

This would be in keeping with the gospel principle, "The first shall be last and the last shall be first." (D&C 29:30)

Where should we be **now**? ? ? I have the impression that there is a time for all things, including particular diets; that our disposition and nature determine the foods we desire and at the same time the food we eat determines our disposition and nature.

An interesting point is put forth by a nutritional doctor concerning fruit. "...I come to the natural conclusion that fruit is the natural food for man. We must consider, however, that a diet consisting entirely of fruit develops a very psychic and sensitive body, which would not be advisable for coarse, undeveloped, undisciplined individuals. One who has refined his body by living on fruits, must have mental control and stability." (Iridology, pg. 337)

This seems to fit in with the pattern of eating fruit in Eden and in the Millennium. On the other hand you think of the diet of savages and barbarians as meat. Does meat create a carnal nature and a carnal nature desire meat? If

so, that would make herbs the diet for the in-betweeners—
those trying to overcome their carnal natures and gain more
spirituality.

These speculations are purely my own and they are
purely speculations.

I feel it is necessary to repent of wrong habits, and
continually strive to learn—and keep—the commandments,
and thus work toward the sanctification which the Lord has
urged the Saints to attain. He has given us the Word of
Wisdom to show us the law by which our bodies may attain
optimum health whereby we may have both the strength to
fulfill all that is required of us and the clarity of mind to be
able to understand that which otherwise would remain a
mystery to us. Living the Word of Wisdom is a great
challenge, upon which rests a greater blessing. Step by step
and day by day we may seek to attain this.

Chapter XIX

REPENTANCE AND
THE WORD OF WISDOM

It is wonderful to realize how the law of repentance applies to the Word of Wisdom. First you must **recognize** that you are not living in full accordance with the Word of Wisdom. Then you must **regret** the things you are doing wrong. Only when you truly regret it will your **resolve** to improve and do what is right be strong enough to bring results. As you **reform** you will replace your harmful habits with good habits that are in accordance with the Lord's will. Since disobedience to the Word of Wisdom is a sin against your own body as well as being an act of disobedience to the Lord, you must **repay** your own body for the harm you have caused it. This happens as the good food you now eat nourishes the body sufficiently for it to build new tissue to replace the old.

Repentance is not painless. You have to pay a price, though not nearly the price equivalent to the sin. When we consider we have been mistreating our bodies for years and years, we must be willing to suffer a few weeks of repayment to receive the Lord's full forgiveness. (What I am referring to here as "repentance" is given other names by various nutritionists and doctors. It might be referred to as the retracing process, a healing crisis, health responses, or a cleansing.)

Because we are all individuals we have different ways of reacting to things. Seldom will two people react in exactly the same way. To give you an idea of how one person experienced this cleansing (repentance) procedure I'd like to relate what happened to a friend of mine. She had been discussing the different points of the Word of Wisdom with me and studying the counsel of Brigham Young and others and decided that this was right and she was going to change. I have seldom seen a person repent so completely and so quickly in something like this. In a matter of just a few weeks she felt and looked just great. She couldn't get over it. Then one morning I got a telephone call from her. She had sores on her face. (She said they looked and felt just like the staph infection she had once had.) These sores lasted a couple of weeks. A few days later she got severe leg cramps. These lasted through one bad night and slowly dwindled away the next day and they were gone. (She used to have leg cramps that would keep her awake night after night over a period of a year or two.) Then she broke out with hives which lasted a couple of days. (She used to have trouble with hives. They would cover her whole upper body.)

But one day she called and asked, "Hey, are **bad habits** supposed to come back too?" Now she had one on me. I had no idea. She said she used to be terrible about biting her fingernails and kept them bitten clear down to the quick. For some reason, here she was biting her fingernails again. This also lasted one day and that was it!

This series of episodes took place in the space of about three weeks. After that she felt wonderful. She was cheerful and lovely. Her figure became slender and trim and she was a ray of smiles and happiness.

If you have been loading your body down with toxic material, impurities, excesses of all sorts, and then you switch over to correct habits, your body is going to undergo some rather definite changes. The overall effect will be good but there may be some pretty painful change-over effects. Don't get discouraged if you seem to be feeling worse instead of better for a while, especially if after you change your diet you get to feeling better and better until Wow! you feel great! Then suddenly, Pow! You start to break out with a rash or a boil here and a pain there and who knows what all begins to take place. Instead of fearing it or thinking you're on the wrong track, rejoice! You are experiencing repentance from the sins you have previously committed against your body through your wrong health habits. Be assured these sudden bad effects will pass quickly, perhaps in just a few days or a week or so. Think of it as all those "bad" things leaving your body and be ready to enjoy the really good, clean health toward which you have been working. (One way you can tell whether you are experiencing a cleansing or if you have simply come down with some disease is by your body's elimination. In a cleansing the elimination systems are working well. In a disease condition you frequently will have either diarrhea or constipation. In a cleansing situation you would have neither of these. Be careful not to mistake a nice, loose bowel movement for diarrhea. When the bowel is eliminating properly, there should be about three bowel movements a day. The stool should be soft and pass easily.)

If you will observe carefully you will probably discover that these aches, pains, rashes or other problems are the same as ones you have experienced before in your life. If you will also notice, these things seem to reappear in the reverse order in which you originally experienced them. When you go through a cleansing of your physical body due to a new and better dietary program, the old problems which you thought you had overcome, but which were really only suppressed, will be eliminated from your body and new, clean, healthy cell tissue will replace the old diseased tissue. As this happens you will experience the same discomfort as when you had the problem, except it will probably be more severe. It will, however, pass very quickly. And it seems to follow the law of the Lord that "the first shall be last, and the last shall be first." (D&C 29: 30)

Don't dwell on this or worry about it, but if and when it does happen to you, you may recognize it as the blessing which it truly is.

HIDDEN TREASURES
TO THE WORD OF WISDOM

Part II

As a frontispiece to this book, a quotation of George Q. Cannon is used, in which he said that if we followed the counsel given in the Word of Wisdom we would receive great treasures of wisdom which would enable us to see a thousand points where we could take better care of our bodies. Part II of this book will demonstrate a few of these points and will suggest sources for your further study, that you may find many great treasures of wisdom to help you to a happier, healthier life.

Chapter I

SPROUTS AND
INDOOR GARDENING

Do you like fresh peas out of the pod? Would you like to have them in December? Then try sprouting mung beans. They taste very much like the tiny fresh peas. And they are remarkably nutritious. In fact, sprouts are probably the most nutritious food you can eat. By taking good-quality seeds and, using the most primitive method of preparation, you can have a food which provides protein, carbohydrates, vitamins and minerals—all of these in the form most perfectly suited to the use of your body.

Whereas persons with health problems very often cannot use some of the whole natural grains, beans, or seeds, they will find that the starch and protein of sprouts from these same foods are readily digested with the help of the high quantity of enzymes they contain. (Cooking destroys many of these essential enzymes.) All sprouts contain Vitamins A, B and C equivalent to those found in fruit. Alfalfa sprouts are also rich in Vitamins D, E, G, K and U. Chickpea sprouts are especially high in protein.

Your sprouting equipment may be as plain or fancy as you wish. There are various sprouters available on the market. Use whatever you wish as long as you follow the principle of thoroughly soaking the seeds, keeping them damp, rinsing them often, and keeping them in the dark until sprouted.

The simplest way I know is to use a plain quart jar. Place a half cup of mung beans, soybeans, lentils, sunflower seeds or chickpeas in a large-mouth jar. If using alfalfa or sesame seed or any other small seeds, use only two tablespoons. Cover with water to about two inches above the seeds or beans. Small seeds should soak in this water for two or three hours. Larger seeds should soak twelve hours or so. With a rubber band or a jar ring, secure wire screening, cheesecloth, nylon net or even nylon stocking over the top of the jar. After soaking the required amount of time, drain off the water. (The soak water contains many of the water-soluble vitamins so try to use it in gravies, sauces, or drinks.) Set the drained jar of beans or seeds on a dark, warm shelf. Rinse three or four times a day to keep moist and fresh, being careful to drain thoroughly each time.

When the sprouts reach the length of the seed they may be eaten. On wheat, do not mistake the three tiny roots for the sprout. The sprout, on the opposite end of the kernel from the little roots, should be the length of the kernel when it's ready to eat. It usually takes takes two or three days, sometimes less. Alfalfa sprouts may continue to grow until they fill the jar, as long as you rinse them and keep them fresh. Then they may be set in the daylight and they will develop chlorophyll, which increases their nutritional value even more. Beans become strong flavored if left to grow too long, so it's best to use them when the sprout is the length of the bean. Mung beans, however, may be left to grow and fill the jar and then used in the various Chinese-type recipes such as salads, egg foo yung, or chow mein. After the sprouts have reached the desired length they may be refrigerated and they will retain their full food value and flavor for sixty to ninety hours.

After you have experimented with sprouting you might like to do a little indoor gardening. Anyone, anywhere, can enjoy the privilege of having fresh produce any time of the year, grown organically, with no chemical fertilizers or insecticides ever touching them, and the saving in food costs will be noticed right away. This food may be raised in your window boxes, trays, shallow dishes, or baking dishes.

The most practical plants to grow are wheatgrass, buckwheat lettuce, sunflower seed greens, and radish greens. They grow in only seven days and may be used plain, or in salads or soups.

Any shallow baking pan or tray will work. You can usually find all you need in second-hand stores or thrift shops for ten to twenty-five cents each. Use the best soil available, preferably compost. Soak the seed overnight. Be sure to put peat moss in the bottom of your container before putting in the earth to assure good ventilation. Wet the soil thoroughly and spread a thick layer of seeds. (The seeds should touch each other.) Cover with about eight thicknesses of wet newspaper. Then place a plastic sheet over that to prevent drying. Set in a dark cupboard or closet. In about three days the growth will begin to lift the newspapers. Remove the plastic sheet and newspaper and place your containers in the sunlight or where there is plenty of daylight. Be sure to water the plants regularly when they begin to grow as there is not enough soil to retain the moisture.

The wheatgrass should reach six to twelve inches before you cut it. It can then be juiced, snipped into soups or salads, or used to purify water. A dish of wheatgrass growing in each room of the house would help to purify and deodorize the air besides being very attractive. If the soil is good a second or third crop of wheatgrass may be grown from the one planting.

Buckwheat lettuce can be eaten as soon as the little leaves are developed and the seed hull falls off. Sometimes you have to remove some of the hulls that remain on the plants. It is usually three or four inches high when it is ready to use. The buckwheat lettuce and the sunflower seed sprouts may be used similarly, either chopped up in salads or snipped off and eaten plain or with a dip. This is also true of nasturtium and radish plants.

Comfrey is a perennial plant which grows indoors as well as outdoors. It is a valuable medicinal herb. The leaves, when used in a poultice, are excellent for taking down swelling or healing a burn. Made into a tea it is good for any stomach upset. It also makes a delicious green drink when blended with water and pineapple juice.

You can also grow the slower maturing plants such as parsley, scallions, celery and dandelions, though they take more time and require some attention.

Other things you might consider would be to plant window boxes or planters with useful herbs or fruit vines. And if recent studies are correct, I would recommend that each morning you say, "Good morning" to your plants, that you never quarrel in front of them and sing a pretty song now and then to help them flourish. If you don't notice any difference in your plants, it will at least be good for you!

Chapter II

SALAD HERBS

Herbs which you have been throwing away but which are both delicious and nutritious are carrot tops, radish tops, turnip and beet tops. The new tender dandelion leaves can be eaten as salad or as cooked greens. And those thistles that are so bothersome? Knock the stickery leaves from the stock and eat it as you would eat celery.

We have taken so many perfectly good herbs and made them unappetizing by our preparation of them. Overcooked spinach is still a very much disliked food by most children in spite of Popeye's efforts to make it appealing. Fresh, tender spinach is delicious when served as a tossed green salad or on a salad tray. And few members of the family even know it is spinach they are eating.

What do you do when you don't have any salad vegetables in the house and your buckwheat lettuce isn't quite ready to eat? One early spring day I was out puttering around the garden spot to see if the ground was dry enough to work-up. It wasn't, but as I sauntered around in the warm sunshine and watched my husband build a compost pit, I noticed several really nice bunches of weeds. I remembered reading in "Eat the Weeds" that a very good salad herb is the common garden weed.[1] Though I couldn't identify the plant by name at that time (later I found out it was Amaranth) I plucked a crisp tender stem and nibbled the leaves. It was very mild and flavorful. I quickly gathered a bowlful and had a fresh salad for lunch. Although it was good as a tossed salad, I really enjoyed eating it more the way I eat buckwheat lettuce. I like to just snip off a few stems and eat them plain or served with a dip.

Later that afternoon we wandered on down to our park area by the creek to see how many other wild herbs were available for eating in the early spring. The stinging nettles were just up, about eight or ten inches high. I carefully (though not carefully enough!) broke off a half dozen or so plants and put them in my basket. Then I grabbed a handful of leaves, rubbed them between my hands so they became slightly juicy, and rubbed them over the places I had been stung by them. Their own juice will counteract the sting, although it leaves a slight numb feeling. Later I rinsed the leaves I had gathered and gently steamed them for two or three minutes. They were delicious. Because they continued to cook another ten minutes before my husband tasted them, they were then bitter and very unpleasant. So steam gently only two or three minutes.

Several areas in the park were carpeted with the tangy clover-leafed sorrel. It's fun to nibble on, but it also adds a tang to tossed salads. The bracken fern was just starting to uncurl. I snipped off the still-curled heads from some of the stalks that were about ten inches high. Since there is varying opinion as to their edibility[2] I took only a few. They were delicious, with the nutty flavor of almonds. We saw other plants that were probably edible but what we can't identify we don't eat. Since that time we have had a botanist come out and identify the various edible plants on our place.

Other wild salad herbs that might be in your locality include: Amaranth (Pigweed), Bedstraw (Goosegrass), Cattail, Chickweed, Dandelion, Hollyhock, Lambsquarters (Wild Spinach), Nasturtium, Peppergrass, and Scurvy Grass.

Chapter III

THERE ARE ALSO
UNWHOLESOME HERBS

When Adam was cast from the Garden of Eden into the cold and dreary world he probably discovered that not all the herbs were wholesome. In fact, in this world there are multitude of unwholesome herbs. And, as with many other things which are bad for us, they often look quite enticing.

The following information was taken from a bulletin (author unknown) which lists some of the more common poisonous plants. There are many, many others, some of which closely resemble good edible plants, so it is important that you be careful in your selection of herbs which you might use for food. When in doubt—don't!

"Information on Common Plant Poisons"

"People may die from eating common plants, including both outdoor plants and those often grown in homes and school rooms.

"Doctors who recently treated a woman patient for seven days after she bit into the stalk of a dieffenbachia bush were amazed to find the plant growing in their own home and in many publc places. This plant is sometimes called dumb cane because the stalk contains crystals of calcium oxalate that become embedded in the tissues of the mouth and tongue, causing severe swelling and striking the victim speechless. Swelling of the base of the tongue could block the air passage to the throat, which would cause death. This plant is also known as elephant ear.

"It really isn't surprising to find poisonous plants in the yard or house since more than 700 species of plants in the United States and Canada are known to have caused death or illness.

"The U. S. Public Health Service reports that about 12,000 children every year chew or swallow potentially poisonous plants. A recent study conducted in a large metropolitan area disclosed that out of 100 child poisonings in the area, 10% of them were caused from eating toxic plants, and more than half of the parents did not realize the plants were dangerous.

"Who would suspect, for instance, the pretty oleander bush which grows indoors could kill a child who merely ate one leaf from the plant. People have died merely from eating steaks that were placed on oleander twigs and roasted.

"Potions from Mountain Laurel were used as a means of suicide by Indians many years ago. One leaf of the poinsetta could kill a child, and tea made from mistletoe berries has killed adults.

"Poison is found in many different types of plants, and those with bright colored berries are often lethal. Fruit trees should also be suspected since twigs of cherry trees release cyanide when eaten."

"The Most Prevalent Poisonous Plants
That Might Grow in or Near Your Home

House Plants

Plant	Toxic part	Symptoms
Hyacinth	Bulbs	Nausea, vomiting, diarrhea. May be fatal.
Narcissus and Daffodil	Bulbs	Nausea, vomiting, diarrhea. May be fatal.
Oleander	Leaves, branches	Extremely poisonous. Affects the heart, produces severe digestive upset and has caused death.
Poinsettia	Leaves	Fatal. One leaf can kill a child.
Dieffenbachia	All parts	Intense burning and irritation of the mouth and tongue. Death can occur if base of tongue swells enough to block the air passage of the throat.
Rosary Pea and Castor Bean	Seeds	Fatal. A single Rosary Pea seed has caused death. One or two Castor Bean seeds are near the lethal dose for adults.
Mistletoe	Berries	Fatal. Both children and adults have died from eating the berries.

Flower Garden Plants

Plant	Toxic part	Symptoms
Larkspur	Young plant, seeds	Digestive upset, nervous excitement, depression. May be fatal.
Monkshood	Flesh roots	Digestive upset and nervous excitement.
Autumn Crocus, Star of Bethlehem	Bulbs	Vomiting and nervous excitement.
Lily of the Valley	Leaves, Flowers	Irregular heart beat and pulse, usually accompanied by digestive upset and mental confusion.

Iris	Underground stems	Severe, but not usually serious digestive upset.
Foxglove	Leaves	One of the sources of the drug digitalis, used to stimulate the heart. In large amounts, the active principles cause dangerously irregular heart beat and pulse, usually digestive upset and mental confusion. May be fatal.
Bleeding Heart (Dutchman's Breeches)	Foliage, roots	May be poisonous in large amounts. Has proven fatal to cattle.

Vegetable Garden Plants

| Rhubarb | Leaf blade | Fatal. Large amounts of raw or cooked leaves can cause convulsions and coma followed rapidly by death. |

Ornamental Plants

Daphne	Berries	Fatal. A few berries can kill a child.
Wisteria	Seeds, Pods	Mild to severe digestive upset. Many children are poisoned by this plant.
Golden Chain	Bean-like capsules in which the seeds are suspended	Severe poisoning. Excitement, staggering, convulsions and coma. May be fatal.
Laurel Rhododendron Azalias	All parts	Fatal. Produces nausea and vomiting, depression, difficult breathing, prostration and coma.
Jasmine	Berries	Fatal. Digestive disturbance and nervous symptoms.

Trees and Shrubs

Wild and cultivated Cherries	Twigs, foliage	Fatal. Contains a compound that releases cyanide when eaten. Gasping excitement and prostration are common symptoms that often appear within minutes.
Oaks	Foliage, Acorns	Affects kidneys gradually. Symptoms appear only after several days or weeks. Takes a large amount for poisoning. Children should not be allowed to chew on acorns.
Elderberry		Children have been poisoned by using pieces of the pithy stems for blowguns. Nausea and digestive upset.
Black Locust	Bark, sprouts, foliage	Children have suffered nausea, weakness and depression after chewing the bark and seeds.

Chapter IV

HERB MEDICINE

My first introduction to herbs was in their usefulness as medicine. I was browsing through my sister's bookshelf and a book called "Back to Eden"[1] caught my eye. As I thumbed through it I was fascinated by the many, many herbs and their many, many uses. Still hoping there might be a help for my dizzy head I skimmed through the index. I saw the word **antispasmodic** and it sounded as if it were what I needed! I read about a most fascinating herb, the lobelia plant. It appeared to be a medicine man's cure-all. When I used it in some of the suggested ways it really did work. Combined with slippery elm bark powder as a poultice it was marvelous for drawing out infection. I made a tea using lobelia and cayenne to see if it could stop my spells. It seemed to work and I got my hopes high. One day I had a small bottle of it in my purse in case I had a spell. During Relief Society one of the sisters had an asthma attack and just coughed and coughed. I remembered reading that the lobelia and cayenne was supposed to work in the case of asthma so I slipped out into the hallway where she had gone, still coughing. I told her about it and offered it to her but she told me she had her pills the doctor had given her. As she searched in her purse she found she didn't have any with her. (Cough! Cough! Cough!) Again I offered the lobelia compound to her and I'm sure it was with grave misgivings, and more to have me leave her alone than because she thought it would help, that she agreed to take some. She drank it down (and looked as if she might lose the top of her head—it's a little bit hot!), and after trying to cool it by taking a drink of water, she returned with me to the Relief

Society lesson. My best friend, who had been studying herbs with me and knew what I was up to when I left the room, could hardly sit still through the rest of the lesson, she was so excited to see that the coughing had stopped completely.

Another friend of mind stayed home from church one Sunday because she had a miserable sore just under her nose. It was fiery red and raw and she said it "hurt like a boil, clear to the bone!" I told her to wet a dab of cayenne and put it on the sore. She looked at me as if I had lost my senses, but the sore hurt so much she figured nothing could hurt much more. She put the cayenne on the sore and her eyes watered as it smarted. But five minutes later the pain was gone and by the next morning the sore was nearly healed.

She became a believer. She gave it to her dad for his ulcers, to her mother for her cold feet, and to her sister for constipation. In addition, when her mother got unpleasant reactions from a diuretic her doctor had prescribed, my friend gave her lobelia instead and it immediately took the water off and there were no bad side effects.

Since then I've wondered if I should avoid the subject when she's around because she starts to sound like an old-time medicine man! I guess when you get results like that it makes you want to get on your soap box and tell everyone about it.

My thirteen-year-old son is pretty easy going, but he constantly hassles me abut the "witch's" medicine I would recommend for this or that problem. But one fateful day he got sick. He came to me looking droopy and complained of being dizzy and not feeling good. He was running a fever and had a rash all over his body. The next day he was to go on an overnight campout with his friends. "Okay, what can I take to get over this by tomorrow?"

Wow! He doesn't expect much, does he? After telling him there was no assurance he'd be able to go on the outing I tried to sound very sure of myself as I told him to take one-half teaspoonful of powdered Vitamin C (1500 mg.) every two or three hours, and a capsule full (00 size—scant ½ teaspoon) of cayenne, drink a cup of peppermint tea and go to bed.

He went on the outing feeling fine the next day. Was it my "witch's" medicine or not? I'll never know, but his attitude certainly changed. He still jokingly teases me about my witch's medicine, but he also comes to me for a "cure" for each of his little physical problems.

There are three reasons that make me feel herb medicine is the best.

1. It is far less expensive than drug-store or prescription medicine.

2. It is "natural" medicine in preference to dangerous drugs, chemicals, and poisons.

3. The Lord says to use it. (D&C 42:43.)

The Prophet Joseph Smith said:

"I preached to a large congregation at the stand, on the science and practice of medicine, desiring to persuade the Saints to trust in God when sick, and not in an arm of flesh, and live by faith and not by medicine, or poison; and when they are sick, and called for the elders to pray for them, and they were not healed, to use herbs and mild food." (DHC VI:414)

Brigham Young taught that the sick should "take a little something to cleanse the stomach, bowels and blood, and wait patiently, and let nature have the time to gain the advantage over the disease. (J.D. 15:225) There are several herbs that will do this for you. One of them that Brigham Young suggested was lobelia. (J.D. 13:275) It was a common use among the Mormon pioneers.

LOBELIA

I'd like to acquaint you a little with **lobelia**. Its botanical name is **Lobelia Inflata,** but its common names give you an idea of what it is used for: wild tobacco, emetic herb, emetic weed, puke weed, asthma weed, gag root, eyebright, vomit wort. (**Back to Eden,** pg. 253-380.) It can be used for an emetic (something to make you vomit), expectorant, diuretic (to increase flow of urine), nervine (to help the nerves, to calm and soothe), diaphoretic (to produce perspiration), and antispasmodic (to relieve or prevent spasms).

Lobelia is a relaxant and should always be used in conjunction with an herb that is a stimulant. Add it to poultices for abscesses and boils. (1/3 lobelia to 2/3 slippery elm bark or other herb.)

Given in small doses it quiets the stomach and will stop spasmodic vomiting, but given in larger doses it will induce vomiting. Used in a tincture it quickly clears the air passages of the lungs. In combination with cayenne and used as an enema it will take care of the most obstinate constipation.

Because it is such a relaxant it has been classed by some in the medical profession as dangerous, but used with cayenne or other stimulants it has wonderful results with no harmful after or side effects.

CAYENNE

Cayenne is the most natural and ideal stimulant in the field of medicine, according to many herbalists. (**Back to Eden**, pg. 215-230) It is non-poisonous and there is no harmful reaction to its use. You might worry that it would burn the sore or the lining of the stomach, but it doesn't. It can be applied directly into a sore, and though it will smart, it causes immediate healing.

It can be used in many ways: in dry powder form, in capsules, as a linament, as a tincture, as a tea, as a poultice, or as a fomentation. The POWDERED cayenne can be placed directly on a sore, whether an open wound or an old ulcer, and the sore will heal in a very short time.

To help stomach ulcers take two No. 00 capsules full of cayenne three times a day. The first few times it may cause a burning sensation or pain, but this only shows that it is getting to the sores. After that you will feel no pain, neither from the cayenne nor from the ulcers. Continue taking it to help the body completely heal the ulcers. (If you don't have the capsules you can mix it in water or make a tea of it or mix it into pieces of bread and roll it into balls and swallow them. It's just more pleasant to take it in the capsules.)

In cases of heart failure cayenne gives the immediate, lasting stimulation which is necessary. Cayenne works first on the heart, then on the arteries, capillaries and nerves.

For a lazy, sluggish feeling such as spring fever, take cayenne and get the circulation going. Take it for scarlet fever, yellow fever, pneumonia, pleurisy, rheumatism, inflammation, colds.

An enema of cayenne with lobelia and slippery elm bark is excellent. Make a tea with a cup of boiling water, ½ teaspoon cayenne and ¼ teaspoon lobelia and 1 teaspoon slipper elm. Cool this down with three cups of water.

POULTICES (Ibid., pg. 216) of cayenne used on the chest or back help break up bad chest congestion. I simply dip strips of sheet in a heavy solution of cayenne in hot water and wrap them around the chest and back. Then wrap a large dry towel around it. It will burn and get fiery red, but within ten minutes of the time it is removed the burn and redness leave. Leave it on ten minutes to one hour, depending on the age of the person. An enema should also be given. The stomach should also be emptied. Vomiting can be induced with ½ to 1 teaspoon each of cayenne and lobelia. This will help in pleurisy, rheumatism, pneumonia, asthma, et cetera.

One LINIMENT (Ibid., pg. 219) you can make is the following: Boil gently for ten minutes one tablespoon of cayenne in one pint of cider vinegar. Bottle it hot and unstrained. Use for congestion, sprains, wounds, bruises, scalds, burns and sunburn. Rinse your mouth with it for help in pyorrhea. Gargle it for any sore throat. Rinse the mouth and apply it to the gums for trench mouth, canker sores, et cetera.

A combination of 2 ounces of gum myrrh, 1 ounce golden seal, and ½ ounce cayenne in one pint raspberry vinegar and one pint water is also a good liniment. (Ibid., pg. 216) This should stand for a week or ten days and should be shaken up each day.

A combination of cayenne and lobelia, whether as a tincture or a tea, will immediately relieve an asthma attack. Though quite unpleasant to take, the results are worth it. Use it in any case of difficult breathing and also for whooping cough.

Don't be afraid to use cayenne. It cannot harm you, no matter how you use it. It is nutritional as well as medicinal, so it can be used daily to keep good tone in the stomach and other organs, improve circulation and repair cell tissues.

You can create your own drugstore right out in your own woods or field. You can make your own salves, liniments, et cetera. You can learn to be self-sustaining so far as your daily problems of sickness and injury are concerned. When you consider the terrible shortage of doctors, and the long wait in the doctor's waiting room, waiting to see the doctor to ask him about some simple problem that is worrying you or making you uncomfortable, it makes good sense to follow the counsel of Brigham Young and start doctoring yourself. He agreed that there was a time and use for doctors, especially the surgeon for setting broken limbs or when surgery is required, but that the women were running to the doctor for all the simple little things they should be able to take care of themselves.

GATHERING HERBS

In order to take care of ourselves we must study and learn about those things which have therapeutic properties and learn to acquire and use them. The medicinal properties of herbs are found in the leaves, flowers, seeds, barks and roots. These must be gathered at the right time of the year and properly cured to produce quality medicine. The ROOTS of annuals should be gathered before they are in flower. The roots of biennials should be gathered in the autumn, after their first year's growth. The roots of perennials should be gathered in the spring, before vegetation has begun. Before they are dried, the solid parts of these roots are to be cut in slices, after being washed.

LEAVES are to be gathered when they are full grown and just before the fading of the flower. Leaves should always be collected in clear, dry weather, in the morning after the dew is off. They are at their best when the flower is in bloom and should be collected at this time. Leaves of biennials are most valuable during the second year of their growth. The best leaves are those that retain their natural green color.

SEEDS are gathered when they are fully ripe. FLOWERS are gathered when they are in their peak or prime.

Herbs should be dried thoroughly, preferably in an airy place in the shade. The sun does hasten drying but it also robs them of some of their value. Drying them in a dehydrator, of course, is the easiest way. After drying they should be placed in heavy paper sacks and hung in a dry place.

PRESERVING HERBS

A DECOCTION is an extract obtained by boiling. To make a decoction from barks and roots cover them with water and let them soak in the refrigerator for eight to ten hours. Then boil vigorously for 15 to 30 minutes. Pour off the liquid and set aside. Cover with fresh water, boil again and pour off the liquid a second time. Combine the liquors and strain through a cotton cloth; place on low heat and reduce to a concentrate.

To make a decoction of the blossoms and leaves, cover the herbs with water and simmer on low heat for two hours. Strain and press. Return liquor to low heat and reduce to a concentrate.

A TINCTURE is a process to preserve herbs in a concentrated form without using heat. For dried herbs use six ounces of cut herb to one quart of apple-cider vinegar. For fresh herbs, pack them into wide-mouth bottle (dark of possible) and cover with vinegar. For dried or fresh, leave in bottle for ten to fourteen days. Shake the bottle up well twice a day. Strain, press, bottle, seal and label. Dark bottles preserve quality better.

To make OILS of HERBS cover herbs with olive oil and let stand ten to fourteen days in a warm place of at room temperature. Press oil from herb and bottle and label. Oil of capsicum (cayenne) is excellent for toothache.

You can make your own HERB SALVE by thoroughly mixing one pound of finely cut herbs, one and one-half pounds of lard, tallow, or lanolin, and four ounces of beeswax. Cover and melt in the heat of the sun or in oven under 200 degrees for three or four hours or until melted. Stir about every hour. Strain, press, place in jar and label. Equal parts white clover and yellow dock make an excellent salve for itches and sores. Chickweek also makes an excellent salve for burns, boils, skin diseases, and all kinds of wounds.

I am not attempting here to say this is all you need for your home medicine chest. What I am saying is that there are many wholesome herbs which the Lord has put here for our use. There are many ways of using them. It is up to us to study it out for ourselves and learn to apply that which we learn.

Chapter V

THE BLESSINGS OF A FAMINE

What a title! How can a famine be a blessing? We could consider D&C 96:3, where the Lord said that all things wherewith we are afflicted shall work together for our good. Can you conceive of some of the blessings then that might come to us as a result of famine?

Heber C. Kimball made the following remarks to the saints in 1854. "I wish many of you had been through the scenes that brother Brigham and many others have.... It will give you an experience that you have not got, and I do not know that you can have it until you have been tried." (J.D. 2:159) So for our own personal growth we must face tribulations and be put to the test as to whether our faith and testimony are enough to keep us true to the faith.

George A. Smith said in 1874:

> "...It has been generally accepted among us that the redemption of Zion would not occur upon any other principle than upon the law of consecration.... We have looked forward to the day when Babylon would fall, when we could not draw our supplies from her midst, and when our own ingenuity, talent and skill must supply our wants." (J.D. 17:59, 61)

As you consider these remarks, think of the experiences related to getting your own food supply on hand as you prepared for future famine or other calamity. Did your Elders' Quorum or Seventies' group work together to secure certain food storage items such as wheat or beans? Did you work together at the canneries to supply the necessary commodities for the welfare program, plus being able to share the excess? Did you teach one another how to use these basic storage items so the fear from uncertainty was done away with? Did you find that it was more economical to buy one hundred pounds of something so two or three of you went together on the expense?

I feel these are all worthwhile experiences to lead us to the point where we could live the law of consecration. As I studied about herbs and their uses I invited others in so I could share these findings with them. I had on hand herbs I had bought in bulk quantities as well as some grains and beans for sprouting. One of the younger women was very anxious to try some of these things but her husband was out of work at the time so she could not afford anything. She however had a talent or two that I could use so we struck up a bargain. She was an artist and did beautiful work, but I didn't feel I could afford to buy the painting I wanted, so I swapped grains and herbs for the painting. She had no wheat grinder either, so I ground the wheat and she'd bake me a loaf of bread when she baked hers. Another of my friends takes care of some of my business letters and such in exchange for herbs, beans, and food supplements. I think this is a tiny bit of how the law of consecration will work.

However, I feel the biggest blessings which will come from a famine condition will be, in relation to our health, in our ability to live the Word of Wisdom more fully. When we are forced to live on the food supply we have stored we may be forced to live on a more healthful diet. This of course depends on what you have included in your food storage plan. Following is a list of the food storage items I feel are worthwhile, as well as some of the reasons I chose these particular items.

WHEAT: Because it is such a complete food, especially when sprouted and uncooked, and because of its long storage life, I place it as the main item in my storage plan. (For the vast variety of ways to use it see **Passport to Survival.**

MUNG BEANS: Because of their high Vitamin C content as well as other important nutrients I place these second in my storage plan. I enjoy the taste and texture and variety of uses of the sprouted mung beans.

SOY BEANS: Because they are a complete protein, and though quite flavorless themselves, they can be flavored up in so many ways I feel they are a basic storage item. They can be used sprouted, cooked, or ground into flour.

BUCKWHEAT: Of all the grains and seeds which can be eaten sprouted, I enjoy the buckwheat lettuce the most as a salad substitute.

OTHER GRAINS—BARLEY, CORN, OATS and RYE: These do not store as long as wheat, but our problem will not be how long we can store them but how much nutrition we can obtain from them and how much variety we can add to our diet. (Take into consideration what animals you will be providing for also.) For flavor and texture I much prefer the long-grain brown rice. And POPCORN is a must on my family's program. As long as there is popcorn to munch on we are happy! All grains must be the whole natural grain. Once the grain has been broken it rapidly loses its food value and is unstable to store.

OTHER BEANS: Though the soybean is probably the most nutritious do not leave out the other beans that your family is used to and enjoys such as KIDNEY, RED, NAVY and LIMA, and other legumes (garbanzos, chick peas, lentils).

SEEDS: By all means have on hand seeds for planting next year's garden. Also have seeds for sprouting or eating plain. One of the most nutritious seeds is the ALFALFA[2] seed. It is the only food I have ever heard of which has an element which can rebuild decayed teeth.[3] It is delicious sprouted and used in salads, soups, or plain. The SESAME

seed in its unhulled form contains ten times more
calcium than cow's milk. SUNFLOWER seeds
are highly nutritious raw or sprouted. Other
seeds that can be used as teas or flavorings, each
having highly nutritious properties, are
CARAWAY, FENNEL, FENUGREEK, and
RADISH. Obviously there are many others but I
have always considered variety in sevens. I feel if
I were to store seven varieties each of seeds,
beans and nuts I would be assured of good
variety, giving adequate nutrition.

NUTS: Nutritionally, the ALMOND is king of nuts. PINE
NUTS are also very good. BRAZIL NUTS,
WALNUTS, FILBERTS, CASHEWS and
PEANUTS are nutritious as well as fun to eat, but
all nuts should be chewed very thoroughly to
make them digestible.

I realize I have deviated from what has become known
as the Basic Four in food storage (wheat, powdered milk,
honey and salt) but I have based my storage plan on what I
feel has been given in the Word of Wisdom. Using the grains,
beans, and seeds in their sprouted form makes them herbs,
which we are to use as our main food item.

As far as HONEY and POWDERED MILK are
concerned, I think they are good if you can afford them, but I
feel the grains and beans are more important. The milk and
honey definitely would make our diets more enjoyable and
make greater variety possible in cooking and baking. So
when you feel you have a sufficient quantity of grains, beans
and seeds on hand, then add the honey, powdered milk and
salt to your storage area.

Since the common table salt is not an organic salt it is
not properly utilized by the body. You should rely on the
natural vegetable salts. If you feel you must have salt as
such in your storage plan, I would strongly recommend sea
salt, which is an organic salt. It costs a little more than the
common table salt, but is still a very inexpensive item as
you consider it in your food storage.

Since in a famine condition there would probably be no fresh fruit available, you will want to always preserve as much fruit and as many vegetables as you can each year. Freezing preserves the most nutrition but your food would be in jeopardy in case of power shortage. Canning would preserve the food for you but would destroy so much of its nutritional value. The one process which both stores well and preserves nearly all the nutritional content of food is dehydrating. Although this can be done by drying the fruits and vegetables in the sun (when the humidity is very low) or with great care using your oven, the most effective and efficient way is in a regular dehydrator. These can be quite simply built or purchased. (See **Passport to Survival,** pg. 96) There are also several companies which have prepackaged dehydrated foods which you could purchase for your food storage. Especially good are the soybean products that can be used as meat substitutes. They have the flavor and appearance of various meats, but are total vegetable protein. Also, a good supply of flavorings will make your storage meals more appealing. These should also be dehydrated, nutritious products, with no harmful additives.

If your situation is such that you could do it, I think it would be a good idea to have your own beehives for honey, chickens for eggs, and a goat for milk. Why a goat? They take less feed to produce more milk. The milk is superior to cow's milk for human use. They are cleaner and more easily kept. They also make good lawnmowers! Of course every family situation is different from that of another family. That is why the church has never set forth a program, as such, of food storage, telling us "what" and "how." We must each figure out our own needs and what is available, and then fulfill our responsibilities in seeing that our own families are provided for and, if possible, have enough extra on hand for others we would like to help. If we do that, I feel certain we will be more worthy of the greatest blessing that would come as a result of a famine or other such condition— that the destroying angel would pass us by.

Chapter VI

WHAT ABOUT FOOD SUPPLEMENTS?

Is the use of food supplements in keeping with the Word of Wisdom? This is considered by many to be a highly controversial subject. To me it is more easily considered as you consider the Word of Wisdom in the "Day-One, Day-Two" system. If we are constantly trying to improve ourselves, and if we feel at a particular time in our progress that food supplements are an improvement then we are justified in using them.

If we are taking harmful substances into our bodies then the use of food supplements can help offset the harmful effects.

The viewpoint that if you eat the right food, supplements are not necessary is well taken if you actually know what the right foods are, if you prepare them properly, if they have been properly grown, and if they are available. In our modern society, it is highly improbable that these conditions can be met.

The danger in food supplements, speaking generally, is in our inability to see the whole picture. We determine what our personal weaknesses or problems are and then try to determine which vitamin or mineral deficiency might be responsible. Then we "supplement" our diet with that particular nutrient. If we don't get the desired results either we claim the particular product is at fault or we study and learn that that particular nutrient is not effective unless another particular nutrient is available at the same time. It can get very confusing. And in some cases it can be hazardous. There are certain supplements that can become harmful to your body if taken without the natural balance of other nutrients being present.

So where does this leave us? If the food we eat can't be counted on to adequately meet our needs and if there are complicated rules about using supplements, what are we to do? My suggestion would be to follow the same rules as are given in the Word of Wisdom, which, to my way of thinking, means natural foods processed in a way so as not to destroy their value.

If the food supplements you are considering are derived from inorganic sources such as chemicals or are referred to as being synthetic vitamins or minerals, then they are not in keeping with the Word of Wisdom, which designates wholesome herbs, fruits, grains and animal products. If your food supplements are taken **from** natural organic sources you are a step ahead but you still have to be careful of the nutritional balance.

The ideal situation is to use food supplements which are simply a concentrated form of wholesome herbs, fruits and grains (wholesome means whole; it is the quality of being whole), where nothing has been removed except the water and cellulose fiber, thus leaving the nutritional balance as nature provided it. These would have to be processed from high-quality, organic-grown produce by a low or no-heat process so no nutrients would be destroyed in the processing. If you take supplements such as this, which provide all the nutrients that your body needs for growth and repair, then your body can choose what it needs for its own particular problems, and if it receives an oversupply of some nutrient which is not needed at that time, it will simply eliminate it from the system.

One of the advantages I see in using supplements is the savings of time and effort. Although good nutrition can be attained by using sprouts, making your own organic garden, and using all foods of highest quality, it does take a lot of

time. In this day and age where there is so much that needs
to be done, it seems that if you can accomplish the same goal
in an easier way, yet following correct guide lines, it should
be done. And, in considering the threat of radiation as
mentioned in the chapter on the Destroying Angel, it seems
imperative to take every precaution possible to protect
ourselves from this menace.

In my own case I was able to alleviate many of my
problems when I began using fresh sprouts daily. But it was
time consuming. When I found I could get the same quality
of nutrition from high quality natural food supplements it
made it much easier. Now when I face a stressful situation
which would tend to bring on my former problem, I greatly
increase the amount of supplements I normally take.

So whether you desire to use food supplements or not is
up to you. But if you do, use the counsel of the Word of
Wisdom as a guide line in choosing the best product.

Chapter VII

WHAT ABOUT
SPECIAL OCCASIONS?

Do you have the problem that as long as you are by yourself you can do things that you know are right, but when you are with other people who don't believe the same as you, it is more difficult to adhere to correct practices? This is often the reason some people drink or smoke. When they are by themselves or with others who have the same standards they are okay, but when they are with others they are afraid of the ridicule for being different, so they indulge.

You will probably find this problem facing you as you try to live the full principle of the Word of Wisdom. Maybe some sample solutions would help you pre-plan what to do in such situations.

We are cautioned not to make a big scene over refusing a drink of tea or coffee. All we need to say is, "No, thank you, none for me," in a very polite voice, and drop the subject. It is not necessary to defend your position or to try to force your point of view on others around you. The same is true in relationship to observing other parts of the Word of Wisdom.

If you are invited to someone's home for dinner you'll certainly not want to offend your hostess by refusing the food she has gone to so much work to prepare. Just see to it that you take only small portions of those things which aren't as good for you and then compliment her on the salads, et cetera, that are good for you. After all, with diet, it's not what you do once in a while, it's what you do most of the time that counts. And remember that it is not necessary to overeat just to be polite!

It is often difficult to select a proper meal from a restaurant menu, but often a dinner salad is very good. It is wise to ask the waitress if you are not quite sure what you will be getting. On one menu I saw what sounded like a nice dish. It said "fresh fruit salad on cottage cheese and crisp lettuce." Just out of curiosity I asked the waitress what kind of fruit it had. She said, "Oh, the usual. Peaches, pears—you know."

"Fresh peaches in April?"

"Yea, you know—in a can."

"You mean canned fruit cocktail?"

"Yeah."

The idea of paying $1.25 for fruit cocktail on cottage cheese didn't appeal to me. For a little more I got their special dinner salad with all kinds of fresh vegetables, boiled eggs, olives, et cetera.

What do you do when it is your turn to entertain? There are two things not to do. One is to prepare something that would be far out of your guests' usual diet and thus cause them to be dissatisfied or uncomfortable. The other is to serve a "regular" meal of spaghetti and meat balls and lots of breads and sweets, which would be against your better judgment.

Select a menu which uses the more commonly accepted foods but make sure you prepare them in the best way. Start with a nice, simple soup such as lentil, split-pea, cream of asparagus or broth with tender, cooked, chopped vegetables. Have an attractive salad, either tossed or individual. For your main dish you could serve either golden baked squash or perhaps baked halibut. Add a couple of vegetables such as fresh asparagus cooked so that it is tender, and maybe fresh or frozen green peas. Make sure you don't overcook these vegetables. If they are cooked until they are just tender they are both more delicious and more nutritious. Fresh fruit with cream or whipped cream tops off the meal. If everything is beautiful and delicious your guest need never know it was also "good for him."

Shortly after my husband was called into the bishopric and became a high priest, a high priests' dinner was planned. Although two of the women in charge were very nutrition-conscious, they decided they should still serve a traditional dinner. So a very lovely dinner of ham (B.Y. "don't eat swine's flesh"), scalloped potatoes (most of the nutrition is near the skin which is peeled away), green beans (canned), tossed salad (the base was head lettuce which not only has far less nutritional value but also has a narcotic which is harmful to the nerves), and for dessert a very rich blueberry cobbler (made with sugar and white flour). The meal was delicious and the men really enjoyed it but I determined that when it was my turn to help put on the dinner I would have a meal just as delicious and at the same time stay within the guide lines of the Word of Wisdom and good nutrition.

My first step was to call my brother-in-law, an avid fisherman, and put in my request for two nice salmon. Since two other gals among the group that would be helping also felt the same as I do about nutrition, I knew I could count on their help. We decided to have a soup made of an imitation chicken broth (all vegetable protein) with chopped carrots, celery and green onions. It only takes 10 minutes to cook this. We'd have a tossed salad with its base of fresh green spinach. Besides the usual tomatoes, radishes, et cetera, we would toss in some sprouted mung beans, being careful not to let any in that hadn't sprouted. (It is very unpleasant to crunch down onto an unsprouted mung bean.)

Removing the skin and bone from the baked salmon, we would lay them open on large platters with lemon wedges and parsley as garnishes. For cooked vegetables we could have broccoli and green peas. Molded fruit salad with honey-sweetened whipped cream would be dessert. They could have their choice of herb tea or juice for their drink. We would also have trays of carrot sticks, celery sticks, olives, avocados, and small dishes of lentil sprouts and mung bean sprouts. The only give-away of who prepared the meal would be the addition of the sprouts. Maybe we should leave them out, but we wanted people to have a chance to taste them and see how good they really are.

The idea wasn't to try to put something over on someone. It's just that when you feel strongly that one thing is good for you, whereas the other is harmful, you should love your neighbor as yourself and be as concerned about his health as you are about your own.

The same rule should apply with your next-door neighbor. I don't feel it is necessary to have coffee on hand for my coffee-drinking neighbors. I can offer a cup of Postum or Pero, or a cup of herb tea (or in the summer, a tall glass of iced herb tea), or a glass of fruit juice. In that way I am not contributing to their coffee habit. The responsibility remains on their own shoulders.

Since there were several of my friends who wanted to know more about sprouting seeds and grains, I decided to hold a class in my home. I invited a few others who I thought would probably be interested. One of these was my older sister. The day after the class I phoned her to get her reaction. What a reaction! She said she was very concerned about my children getting to eat nothing but sprouts! (I still haven't exactly figured out how she got that impression.) Then she asked what my poor children were going to have for happy memories if I wouldn't let them have pies and cakes, etc. (This again was not exactly a true situation because I do not refuse to allow my children to eat these things—I just don't prepare them myself.)

But she had a valid point. It is necessary that we build pleasant memories for our children. But I don't think it is necessary to compromise principles in order to do this. When we take something away that is pleasurable, we must be careful to replace it with something else that is also pleasurable. If you decide to knock out the standard birthday cake, make sure you don't knock out the whole birthday. There are many delicious baked goods you can make with natural, whole-grain products. Or you can offer treats which are both delicious and fun. A few suggestions might be: Fruit-Yogurt Shakes, Coconut Balls, Popcorn Treats, or a variety of wholesome hors d'oeuvers. Use your imagination. There is a world of variety around you. Traditions are good. They give us a sense of security. But if the traditions are in opposition to that which is good for you, you must create new traditions based on sound principles.

What about such traditional things as Thanksgiving and Christmas dinners? Reflect for a moment on these occasions in your family. One particular Thanksgiving comes to my mind. It was when I was a child and all the relatives had come to Granny's house for Thanksgiving dinner. The day was perfect, just like Thanksgiving day should be. The air was crisp and fresh, the sun shining brightly and all the cousins were out playing in the garden and orchard area, which had again yielded its harvest of fruit and vegetables. Then came the call to dinner and we rushed in to wash up and be seated around the several tables which had been pushed together. The table was laden with the large turkey and all that goes with it. And we ate, and ate—and ate. I remember the heavy bent-over feeling as I left the table. I don't remember that we raced out to play. It seems as if we sort of hung around or lay down on the grass. I know many of the men found shady places and lay down and went to sleep. The women, of course, who had already been in the kitchen all day preparing the meal, had to return to the kitchen and, with the enlistment of the older girls, do the huge mound of dishes. But then I remember the lines started forming for the bathroom! It seemed as if all afternoon people were waiting to get to the bathroom.

The memory always recalls it in the same way—from brisk, fresh morning to uncomfortable, lethargic afternoon.

Now I look back considering other such Thanksgiving days and I wonder if this is really the way to show our thanks to God for a bounteous harvest. It is true that at the first

Thanksgiving when the pilgrims invited the Indians to the
feast there were tables laden with turkeys and corn and
other bounties of the harvest. But I have a feeling that with
the many people at that feast there were probably not the
huge quantities per person that we too often see at our own
Thanksgiving dinners. We load our own tables down with
food to resemble the Thanksgiving feast pictures we've seen
but we forget to invite the Indians!

Read the words of Elder George Q. Cannon delivered at
General Conference April 7th, 1868, and then consider your
Thanksgiving dinners:

> "God has given to us a land that is bounteous; every
> variety of food can be produced here in the greatest
> profusion. It only requires the exercise of the powers with
> which we are endowed, with proper industry, to bring forth
> food in the greatest abundance and supply every want of
> man and beast. But whilst I speak in this strain about a
> variety of food, I am opposed in my own feelings, to a great
> variety of food at one meal. I believe that we enslave our
> women; we crush out their lives by following the
> pernicious habits of our forefathers in this respect. We sit
> down to table, and, especially if we have friends, our tables
> are covered with every delicacy and variety that we can
> think of. I believe in variety at different meals, but not at
> one meal. I do not believe in mixing up our food. This is
> hurtful. It destroys the stomach by overtaxing the
> digestive powers; and in addition to that it almost wears
> out the lives of our females by keeping them so closely
> confined over cooking stoves. A variety of food is not
> incompatible with simplicity of cooking; they can go hand
> in hand. We can have a diet that will be easily prepared,
> and yet have it healthful. We can have a diet that will be
> tasteful, nutritious and delightful to us, and easy to digest;
> and yet not wear out the lives of our mothers, wives,
> daughters and sisters in its preparation.

> "...We can therefore, if we so please, accommodate
> ourselves to new habits—habits recommended and taught
> to us by the servants of God. One of the great advantages
> that would result from our having a more simple diet would
> be that we should be less apt to overload our stomachs
> through the tempting character of the food we eat. How
> often is the case, after we have eaten enough, somebody

will say, 'Here is something I would like you to eat a little of; do taste it.' Well, you taste, and before you are aware of it, you have eaten more than you should; your stomach rebels, and you feel that you have done a wrong, and if your stomachs are weak, you have to pay the penalty of your imprudence.'' (J.D. 12:223)

Brigham Young said, "No matter whether it is a child or a middle-aged person, whenever the stomach is over-loaded and charged with more than is required, it creates a fever, this fever creates sickness, until death relieves the sufferer. (J.D. 19:68)

Let's reconsider our traditional dinners for special occasions and use prudence in the planning of them that they may truly be meals of thanksgiving.

Chapter VIII

FAVORITE MENUS
AND RECIPES

Have fun creating your own nutritious meals and treats. There are many cook books devoted to health-giving menus and recipes. Adapt them to your desires or use them as guides in discovering new ways to please your family as you look after their health.

There is a bonus benefit from using whole, natural fruits, vegetables, and grains—there is seldom a failure. Lack of a particular ingredient or inaccurate measurement seldom affects the finished product. It's fun to experiment, but really, the best-tasting foods are the simplest. Try different dried or fresh herbs in your bean or grain casseroles. Just a pinch will make a flavor difference. Substitute barley or rice in some of your regular macaroni or noodle dishes. Or try making your own noodles from soybean flour. Try different blends of home-ground flour—see the texture difference.

I would like to share with you a few of the menus and recipes my family enjoys.

BREAKFAST

Using Whole Grains for Breakfast

Grains to use: Wheat (soak overnight), rice, millet, or barley.

Steamed: Use 3½ parts water to 2½ parts grain, and salt to taste, in top of double boiler. Bring water in bottom of double boiler to boil, then turn down to simmer. Steam about 4 hours or until tender. (In her book, "**Passport to Survival**," Esther Dickey says wheat cooked for 14 hours in a stainless steel pan on simmer in the top of a double boiler was planted, and grew!)

or: Add one part grain to two parts cold water, salt to taste; bring to boil, reduce heat and simmer ½ hour or longer depending on grain. (Wheat takes longest.)

Cracked Wheat or Barley Cereal: Bring 3 cups of water, 1 tsp. salt to boil. Sprinkle in one cup coarsely ground wheat. Reduce heat, cover, and simmer for ½ hour. Gently stir twice during cooking.

Rolled Cereal Grains for Breakfast

Grains to use, alone or in combination: Corn meal, fine-ground wheat, rice or barley. Bring 3 cups water to boil. Stir 1 cup meal and 1 tsp. salt into 1 cup cold water until there are no lumps. Then stir it slowly into the boiling water, cover and simmer 5 or 10 minutes.

Family-Favorite Granola

Spread five cups of oatmeal in a large, low pan (broiler pan, sweetroll pan, etc.). Put in a 300 degree oven and brown it very lightly, stirring frequently so it all gets slightly browned. Take from oven and stir in 1 cup each of any or all of the following: wheat germ, rolled wheat, rye flakes, sesame seed, flax seed, slivered nuts, coconut, raisins, currants, or other dried fruits. Warm ½ cup saffola or other oil, and ½ cup honey, till they mix together easily. Pour over the cereal mixture, stirring so no particles are left dry and none are left in lumps. Store in covered jars or in plastic bags. (If you get a chance to store it, that is! It seldom lasts that long at my house!) For something new, use fruit juice instead of milk on it. Grape, pineapple, or apple are especially good.

Breakfast Special

Granola with fresh strawberries on it, whipped cream and a sprinkling of granola on top.

Quick and Cool

Sprouted wheat, coconut, and sliced bananas served with or without milk or cream.

Fancy and Fruitful

Cantaloupe with whipped cream and blueberries.

Special-Blend Flour

For a flour that makes delicious, light pancakes, muffins, or bread, grind together 4 parts wheat, 1 part each of barley, rice and soybeans.

Pancakes

Combine 1½ cups blended flour, ¼ cup powdered milk, 1 tbsp. baking powder, 1 tsp. salt. Beat together 1 egg, 1 cup water, ¼ cup honey, and ¼ cup oil. Stir into dry ingredients. Add a little more water if necessary for right consistency. (If you are out of eggs increase amount of baking powder a little.) Serve with honey-maple syrup (½ cup boiling water, ½ tsp. maple flavoring, ½ cup honey) or fruit syrup (½ cup frozen puree of berries, cherries, etc., ½ cup boiling water, ½ cup honey.).

Muffins

Use pancake recipe, increasing amount of flour by ½ cup.

If you want muffins but are out of eggs, again try these: Combine 2/3 cup rice flour, 1 1/3 cups barley flour, 2 tbsp. baking powder, ½ tsp. salt, ½ cup powdered milk; stir together and add to dry ingredients ¼ cup honey, 1½ cups water, 2 tbsp. oil. Fill greased muffin pan 2/3 full and bake at 400 degrees for 25 to 35 minutes or until golden brown.

A nice cup of herb tea is always pleasant before or with breakfast.

100% Whole-wheat or Special-Blend Bread

8½ to 9½ cups flour

4 tsp. salt

2 pkgs. yeast

1½ cup milk

1½ cup water

1½ cup honey

6 tbsp. oil

Mix 3 cups flour, salt, and undissolved dry yeast. Heat milk, water, honey and oil in sauce pan over low heat until warm. Add to dry ingredients gradually and beat at medium speed, scraping bowl frequently. Add 1 cup flour and beat at high speed 2 minutes, scraping bowl. Stir in enough other flour to make soft dough. Turn out on lightly floured board. Let rest 10 minutes with bowl turned on top. Knead until smooth and elastic, about 10 minutes. Place in greased bowl, turning to grease top. Cover; let rise in warm place until double, about 50 minutes. Punch and let rise again. Punch, turn out on board, divide, shape into 2 loaves, cover and let rise about 50 minutes. Bake at 375 degrees for 35 or 40 minutes.

Mid-Morning Break

For a mid-morning pickup enjoy one of the following: herb tea (hot or iced with lemon and honey), cup of broth, vegetable juice, fruit juice, green drink, or fresh fruit or vegetable sticks.

Lunch Time

My favorite lunches consist of any one or a combination of soup, salad, muffins, or bread. The variety possible is nearly limitless. Use your imagination and fresh, whole, natural products for delicious variety. A few examples which I particularly enjoy are:

Salads: Shredded greens, avocado slices, cottage cheese, sesame seeds. Greens, tomato wedges, green pepper strips, cucumber rings, sliced hard-boiled egg, plain or with favorite dressing. Coleslaw with minced apples, celery, and raisins.

Soups: Broths, plain or with vegetables or grains. Creamed soups. (Put vegetables through blender or Champion juicer; heat and add milk or cream. Add fresh or dried herbs for variety.)

Sandwiches: Although sandwiches using vegetable fillings are in keeping with the rule of separation of proteins and starches, regular protein-filled sandwiches, i.e., meat, egg, cheese, are not. So if you want a protein sandwich, instead of using bread, use a Romaine lettuce leaf. Just place or spread your filling on the leaf, add a dressing if you wish, roll it up and eat it. Try it! You'll like it! Fun for lunch boxes too. Some suggested fillings: Egg salad, tuna salad, cheddar cheese and celery, cottage cheese and chives. Use your imagination.

Supper Suggestions

1. Soup: Chicken broth (all vegetable protein broth that has the flavor of chicken.

>   Entree: Fish (baked, fish sticks, broiled).

>   Salad: Fresh vegetable tray.

2. Egg Foo Yung: Make an omelette of eggs, bean sprouts, green onions, and celery. Thicken beef broth for gravy. Serve with combination tea (comfrey, red clover, nettle, raspberry) and a tossed salad.

3. T.V.P.* Chow Mein: Soak ½ cup pork-flavored T.V.P., in 2 cupes of water to reconstitute. Gently steam 1 cup sliced celery and ½ cup onions in enough water to cover bottom of pan. Add T.V.P., 2 cups fresh bean sprouts, and 1 tbsp. beef flavoring and gently cook for ten minutes. Stir and dissolve 2 heaping tbsp. arrowroot powder or corn starch in ½ cup water and add to sauce to thicken. Serve plain or over dry noodles.

4. Baked squash with butter. (Try a pinch of dried mint some time!) Cooked asparagus or spinach; raw vegetable tray and dip.

5. Baked potato, green beans with onions and T.V.P. bacon bits, tossed salad, fruit-juice punch.

6. Tacos: Ground-beef T.V.P. made "hot" with cayenne; sprouted spanish red beans, cooked until tender, and mashed; diced tomatoes (fresh, canned, or reconstituted dried diced tomatoes); onions, grated cheese, greens (spinach, romaine, water cress), taco shells.

*T.V.P. is total vegetable protein. It is made from soy flour and comes in several meat flavors: beef, pork, chicken, bacon, ham, tuna, shrimp.

7. Soybean Stew: Soak and sprout 2 cups soybeans. Cook about 1½ hours. Add quart of canned tomatoes, ½ cup each celery and onions (or reconstituted dried vegetables) and ½ cup ham-flavored T.V.P. Or make it into a casserole with grated cheese on top.

8. Chili Con Carne: Soak and sprout 2 cups kidney (or other beans. Cook 1½ hours or until crunchy tender. Add dried chili mix, tomato sauce and 1 cup ground-beef T.V.P.

9. Pizza: Make a biscuit dough of whole-wheat flour, and pat into bottom of cookie sheet. Crimp an edge up around it. Spread with pizza sauce, sprinkle on grated cheese, decorate with reconstituted ham-flavored T.V.P. Bake in 400 degrees oven until crust is browned and cheese melted.

10. A special treat for our family is when my husband cooks mushrooms. He gathers a nice panful of the golden chanterelle mushrooms from the woods, thoroughly washes them and slices them into bite-size pieces. He slices one or two large onions and sautes them slowly in butter (about ½ hour). Then he adds the mushrooms, puts a lid on them and lets them slowly steam until tender. He adds water when necessary to maintain a sauce. Then he salts and peppers them to taste (which is quite hot) and adds about ¼ cup vinegar and ½ cup catsup and lets them continue to slowly simmer until the flavors blend (about 1 hour). Just before serving he thickens the sauce with flour. A salad and bread and butter complete the meal. It is delicious.

12. My daughter found an excellent substitution for the above menu when she was experimenting with squash one evening. She sauted the onions the same way. Then instead of mushrooms she used the small yellow summer squash, slicing it up seeds and all. She also added a few spices such as thyme and oregano, but the rest of the recipe was basically the same.

Recipes from a Delicious
Relief Society Luncheon

Baked Zucchini: Parboil sliced zucchini and onion in salted water. Place in casserole. Salt and pepper. Dribble melted butter over it. Use 3/4 cup chopped sweet pickled peppers. Cover with sliced fresh tomatoes or canned tomatoes. Cover top with grated jack cheese. Bake at 375 degrees until cheese is melted.

Creamed Cucumbers: Cube cucumbers and parboil in salted water. Make cream sauce of 2 tbsp. flour, 2 tbsp. butter and 2 cups milk. Add dill weed to sauce to taste.

Jello with Sour-Cream Sauce; Lime jello with sliced bananas, pineapple chunks and marshmallows. Topping: Thicken pineapple juice with cornstarch like a pudding. Fold in sour cream and spread over jello.

Serve with whole-wheat muffins with ground-up raisins and nuts stirred into the batter.

Refreshing Drinks

Yogurt Shakes: 1 cup frozen orange-juice concentrate, ½ cup plain yogurt, ½ cup powdered milk, 1 quart whole raw milk, egg or egg yolk if you wish, and/or protein powder. Blend in blender.

Green Drink: Blend fresh greens (comfrey, parsley, celery, spinach alone or in combination) with water in blender or juicer. Strain and mix half-and-half with unsweetened pineapple juice.

Fruit Drink: 1 can unsweetened pineapple juice, ¼ cup (more or less) Instant Protein, Tiger's Milk, etc.

Special Treats

Coconut Balls: Grind together raisins and/or seeded figs, dates, currants, almonds, brazil nuts and/or filberts. Add a little water if necessary. Then add coconut, rolled wheat and sesame seeds. Roll into 1-inch balls and roll the balls in macaroon coconut.

Popcorn Treats: For popcorn variety add nuts and pour over a syrup of honey or unsulphured molasses and butter to make a carmel-corn.

Dried Fruits: Dried sliced bananas are a wonderful substitute for candy bars. Home-dried fruits are the tastiest, chewiest treats you can serve. To really please guests, or add a touch of the unusual at a potluck picnic or supper, fix a dried Fruit Salad dish. On a lazy susan or large tray, arrang dried pineapple spears, banana slices, pear slices, apple rings, apricots and tiny fruit-leather curls. Your children and your guests will love them. Dried fruits are an excellent addition to any lunch box. You need not add any glaze or preservative of any kind when drying fruits and vegetables. Simply wash them thoroughly, pit or core them, slice them and place one layer of fruit on each drying tray and place them in the dehydrator at 120 degrees. Most fruits are done in about 8 to 24 hours. Dehydrators are inexpensive if you use scrap lumber and get your element, fan and thermostat from second-hand stores. Plans for dehydrators are available at most county extension service centers.

Chapter IX

FUN THINGS

Slant-Board Exercises: Lay on a grassy slope and do them as you breathe deeply of fresh air.

Vacation Time: Make it a health retreat. Deliberately do things that are good for you. Hike, swim, get into clear, fresh air, eat off the land, study and commune with nature. No hot dogs or hamburgers this time!

Make a Rock Rug: Collect small round river rocks ½ to 1½ inches in diameter. Mold them into an 18 x 24-inch "rug" by casting them in clear or colored resin to create a surface similar to a rocky beach. Place in front of your sink so you can do your own foot reflexology as you do the dishes.

Skin Brushing: For that rosy glow of health, briskly brush your body with a vegetable brush or special skin brush. This removes the acid flakes from your skin, increases blood circulation and thus improves the elimination of toxic material from your body through the skin. Brush until you tingle and have a rosy glow all over your body. (It takes about 3 minutes.)

Turn Showering into Massage Time: Take a hot shower, massaging your body thoroughly with the heel of your hand. Massage scalp firmly with fingertips. Learn particular reflex points for most benefit. (Don't use soap—it robs skin of oil and softness. Other products are available that clean but don't remove the natural oil.) Gradually cool the water until it is cold enough to make you catch your breath. This closes the pores, besides being a good stimulant and waker-upper!

Play on the Beach: To increase blood circulation wade in the icy water and then walk in the hot sand alternately for about ten minutes.

Commune with Nature: Spend as much time as you can with nature, learning her ways, resting in her solitude, being invigorated by her freshness. Learn to enjoy her crashing waves, rushing rivers, and babbling brooks. Feel the immensity of her giant forests—the fragile beauty of her delicate violets. Bask in her warm sun and lift your face to her gentle rain. Never be too busy to study the lessons she teaches us as the seasons come and go. Let her teach you about yourself.

Relax: Learn to live life one day at a time. Study, pray, and set your goals. Then relax and allow each day to bring more joy, happiness and blessings into your life.

Chapter X

HOW TO HAVE
A HAPPY, HEALTHY DAY

It is helpful when you begin a new program to outline what you plan to do. An outline similar to the following could be useful. Design it with your personal desires and needs in mind, and for your own health, happiness and spiritual progress.

Upon awakening: A glass of water with either lemon juice or liquid chlorophyll.

Five minutes of reading the scriptures.

First exercise (on your knees!): Personal morning prayer.

Fifteen minutes of slant-board exercises.

Fifteen minutes of rest on slant board. Time may be used in meditation or goal setting.

Skin brushing to cleanse the skin, increase circulation.

Shower: Start with the water hot; end shower by cooling water until it makes you catch your breath.

Breakfast: Cup of herb tea and/or dish of fresh fruit.

Mid-morning: Health drink or snack.

Lunch: Salad of cottage cheese with fresh fruit or raw vegetables.

During the day: Enjoy the beauties of nature, good music, the love of family and friends, the challenge of work.

Half an hour before dinner: Juice or herb tea.

Dinner: A protein OR starch food with salad, soup, vegetables.

Before bed: Read the scriptures.

Evening exercises (on your knees!): Express gratitude for life.

Chapter XI

FOOD FROM THE TABLE OF THE LORD

The Lord has filled the earth with beautiful as well as delicious and nutritious things to eat. Here are some of the bountiful gifts He has given us from which we may select our diet.

Fruits	Vegetables	Grains	Seeds	Dairy Products
Grapes	Beets	Wheat	Pinto beans	Marjoram
Pineapples	Carrots	Oats	Navy beans	Camomile
Apples	Cauliflower	Barley	Spanish red beans	Dairy
Pears	Celery	Rice		Products
Plums	Onions	Millet	Seeds	Whole raw milk
Peaches	Radishes	Rye	Sunflower	Cream
Apricots	Turnips	Buckwheat	Sesame	Butter
Cherries	Spinach	Corn	Pumpkin	Cottage cheese
Strawberries	Bibb lettuce	Nuts	Alfalfa	Cheddar cheese
Blackberries	Romaine	Almonds	Radish	Yogurt
Raspberries	Cabbage	Pine nuts	Poppy	Whey
Loganberries	Cucumbers	Filberts	Caraway	Buttermilk
Avocados	Peppers	Pecans	Fenugreek	Eggs
Currants	Peas	Brazil nuts	Fennel	Other
Cranberries	Green beans	Peanuts	Herbs	Honey
Papayas	Kohlrabi	Cashews	Parsley	
Oranges	Parsnips	Walnuts	Spearmint	
Grapefruit	Potatoes	Coconuts	Peppermint	
Lemons	Squash	Legumes	Red clover	
Limes	Yams	Peas	Red raspberry leaf	
Bananas	Corn	Lentils	Alfalfa	
Blueberries	Broccoli	Soybeans	Papaya	
Figs	Asparagus	Mung beans	Comfrey	
Dates	Artichokes	Garbanzos	Nettle	
Melons	Brussels	Kidney beans		
Tomatoes	sprouts	Lima beans		

Chapter XII

RECOMMENDED READING

There are a thousand and more ways to improve our health. We are counselled to "seek out of the best books words of wisdom." The following books contain some of these words of wisdom. Though you may disagree with some of the concepts presented, as I sometimes do, they can nevertheless be beneficial to you as you study them in your pursuit of knowledge concerning health and happiness.

NUTRITION

Chlorophyll, Nature's Green Magic, Theodor M. Rudolph, $1.25.

Diet for a Small Planet, Frances Lappe, $1.25.

A Doctor's Proven Cure for Arthritis, Geraud Campbell, $6.95.

Essene Gospel of Peace, Edmond B. Szekely, $1.00.

Feel Like a Million, Cathryn Elwood, $.95.

Health Magic Through Chlorophyll, Bernard Jensen, $3.95.

Helping Your Health with Enzymes, Carlson Wade, $1.95.

JM's Nutritional Review, JM Publishing Co., Bismark, N.D., 50¢ an issue.

Let's Eat Right to Keep Fit, Adelle Davis, $1.75.

Let's Get Well, Adelle Davis, $1.95.

Let's Have Healthy Children, Adelle Davis, $1.75.

Let's Live Magazine, monthly publication, $.600 a year.

Nutrition Against Disease, Roger Williams, $7.50.

You Can Master Disease, Bernard Jensen, $3.75.

MEAL PLANNING AND RECIPES

Blending Magic, Bernard Jensen, $3.95.
Creating a Magic Kitchen, Bernard Jensen, $1.95.
Diet for a Small Planet, Frances Lappe, $1.25.
Let's Cook It Right, Adelle Davis, $1.50.
Love Your Body, Viktoras Kulvinskas, $1.25.
Natural Foods Cookbook, Jean Hesitt.
Passport to Survival, Esther Dickey, $3.95.
Vital Foods for Total Health, Bernard Jensen, $4.95.
Wheat for Man, Rosenvall, Flack, Hill, $1.95.

HERBS

Back to Eden, Jethro Kloss, $2.00.
Eat the Weeds, Ben Charles Harris, $3.95.
Kitchen Medicines, Ben Charles Harris, $.75.
Nature's Medicines, Richard Lucas, $.95.

HEALTHY ATITTUDES

The Bible
Book of Mormon
Doctrine and Covenants
Pearl of Great Price
Spiritual Roots of Human Relations, Stephen Covey, $4.95.
I Feel Wonderful—So Can You, Bernard Jensen, $3.95.
Psycho-Cybernetics, Maxwell Maltz, $1.25.
Reflections on a Philosophy, Forrest Shaklee, Sr., $1.00.

SLANT BOARD EXERCISES

A New Slant on Health and Beauty—Slant Board, Bernard Jensen, $1.00.

FOOT REFLEXOLOGY

Helping Yourself With Foot Reflexology, Mildred Carter, $2.45.
Stories the Feet Can Tell, Eunice Ingham, $3.50.

IRIDOLOGY

Science and Practice of Iridology, Bernard Jensen, $15.00.

ORGANIC GARDENING

The Basic Book of Organic Gardening, Robert Rodale, $1.25.

WORD OF WISDOM

The Word of Wisdom, John A. Widtsoe.
Walking in Obedience, Lander.

FOOTNOTES TO PART I

Chapter II

HOW DO WE
PRACTICE THE PRINCIPLE?

1. Improvement Era, 1956, pg. 78, (statement by Joseph Fielding Smith).

2. **Improvement Era**, 1965, pg. 759, (statement by Joseph Fielding Smith).

3. Journal of Discourses 12:221. Also John A. Widtsoe, Joseph Smith—Seeker After Truth, pg. 201.

4. Journal of Discourses, 12:37.

5. Journal of Discourses, 19:68.

6. Journal of Discourses, 12:223.

7. Bernard Jensen, D.C., N.D., **The Science and Practice of Iridology**, (Bernard Jensen Products Pub. Div., Escondido, California, 1952), pg. 342.

Chapter VI

ALL WHOLESOME HERBS

1. **Iridology,** pg. 338.

2. Bernard Jensen, **Vital Foods for Total Health** (Escondido, California, 1965), pg. 29, 431.

3. Ibid: foreword to book.

4. Adelle Davis, **Let's Get Well** (N.Y., Harcourt, Brace & World, 1965), pg. 29, 431.

Chapter IX

AND IT IS PLEASING UNTO ME

1. Harrison Wellford, "Cancer-Causing Chemicals in Meat?" **The Atlantic Monthly,** October 1972, (as condensed in **The Reader's Digest,** December 1972, pg. 134-138).

Chapter X

STAFF OF LIFE

1. Vernice G. Rosenball, Dora D. Flack, Mabel H. Hill, **Wheat for Man,** (S.L.C., Utah; Bookcraft, 1972).

2. Theodore M. Rudolph, Ph.D., **Chlorophyll, Nature's "Green Magic",** (San Gabriel, California: Nutritional Research Publishing Co., 1957), pg. 2.

Chapter XI

WALKING IN OBEDIENCE

1. Adelle Davis, **Let's Get Well**, pg. 340-341, 436.
2. Ibid., pg. 423-426.
3. Caution: Taking a particular B Vitamin by itself can produce deficiencies of the B Vitamins not supplied. It is best to use B Vitamins in a natural balance (as nature supplies them).

Chapter XIII

TREASURES OF KNOWLEDGE

1. **Iridology**, pg. 336.
2. Ibid., pg. 170-171.

Chapter XIV

RUN AND NOT BE WEARY

1. **Reader's Digest**. Also **Iridology**, pg. 170-171.
2. Bernard Jensen, **A New Slant on Health and Beauty— Slant Board** (Escondido, California: Bernard Jensen Products).

Chapter XV

THE DESTROYING ANGEL

1. Gerald M. Lund, **Coming of the Lord** (Salt Lake City: Bookcraft, 1972), pg. 30.

2. G. Edward Griffin, **World Without Cancer,** Westlake, Ca.: American Media)

3. **Cancer News Journal—Voice of the International Association of Cancer Victims and Friends** (Solona Beach, California). An interview with Wm. Donald Kelley, B.A., D.D.S., M.S., F.I.C.A.n., author of **One Answer to Cancer.**

4. Geraud W. Campbell, D.O., with Robert Stone, **A Doctor's Proven Cure for Arthritis,** (West Nyack, N.Y.: Parker Publishing Co., 1972), as quoted in **Let's Live** Magazine, October 1973, pp. 41, 42.

Chapter XVI

THE DESTROYING ANGEL: IATROGENIC DISEASE

1. **Iridology**—introduction.

2. Ibid.

3. Roger Williams, **Nutrition Against Disease** (N.Y.: Pitman Publishing Corp., 1971), pp. 3-19.

4. Pamphlet, "Drug Caused Diseases," H. B. Publications.

5. Editorial note, **Let's Live** magazine, (L.A., California: Oxford Industries), Feb. 1973.

Chapter XVII

THE DESTROYING ANGEL: ENVIRONMENTAL DISEASE

1. A series of articles by Linda Clark entitled "Today's Threat: Environmental Disease" as printed in the **Let's Live** magazine, January-August 1973.

2. Ibid: Jan. 1973, pg. 81.

3. Ibid: Feb. 1973, pg. 79.

4. Mira Louise, **Survival in the Atomic Age**, as quoted in Let's Live magazine, Feb. 1973, pg. 79.

5. Ibid.

FOOTNOTES TO PART II

Chapter II

SALAD HERBS

1. Ben Charles Harris, **Eat the Weeds,** (Barre, Mass.: Barre Publishers, 1971), pg. 61, 138.

2. Ibid: pg. 79.

Chapter IV

HERB MEDICINE

1. Jethro Kloss, **Back to Eden,** (N.Y.: Lancer Books, Inc., 1971.)

Chapter V

THE BLESSINGS OF A FAMINE

1. Esther Dickey, **Passport to Survival** (Salt Lake City, Utah: Bookcraft).

2. **Eat the Weeds,** pg. 56-60.

3. Viktoras Kulvinskas, M.S., **Love Your Body,** (Boston, Mass.: Hippocrates Health Institute, 1972), pg. 80.

4. Ibid: pg. 81

APPENDIX

Excerpts from **The Journal of Discourses** of speeches and sermons delivered by President Brigham Young, his counsellors, the Twelve Apostles, and others on the Word of Wisdom and related subjects.

APPENDIX

Excerpts from The Journal of Discourses

Vol. II, 17-18 by Brigham Young, July 24, 1854:

I could say many things that would be of great worth to you, pertaining to the rising generation, had I time; but I wish to recollect and practise this one item I have briefly laid before you. I wish the daughters of Israel to far exceed their mothers in wisdom. And I wish these young men and boys to far exceed their fathers. I wish my sons to far exceed me in goodness and virtue. This is my earnest desire concerning my children, and that they not only walk in the footsteps of their father, but take a course to enjoy life, health, and vigor while they live, and the Spirit of intelligence from God, that they may far outstrip their father in long life, and in the good they will perform in their day. What I say of my children I will apply to all.

Young men, my young brethren, will you accept a little counsel from me? When you go from this Tabernacle make a covenant with yourselves that you will taste no more ardent spirits, unless it is absolutely necessary, and you know it is; also make a covenant with yourselves that no more of that filthy, nasty, and obnoxious weed called tobacco shall enter your mouths; it is a disgrace to this and every other community. I am well aware of the reflections of many upon this subject. You may say to yourselves, "If I can do as well as my parents, I think I shall do well, and be as good as I want to be; and I should not strive to excell them." But if you do your duty you will far excell them in everything that is good—in holiness, in physical and intellectual strength, for this is your privilege, and it becomes your duty. Young men, take this advice from

me, and practise it in your future life, and it will be more
valuable to you than the riches of this world. "Why,"
say you, "I see the older brethren chew tobacco, why
should I not do it likewise?" Thus the boys have taken
licence from the pernicious habits of others, until they
have formed an appetite, a false appetite; and they love
a little liquor, and a little tobacco, and many other
things that are injurious to their constitutions, and
certainly hurtful to their moral character. Take a
course that you can know more than your parents. We
have had all the traditions of the age in which we were
born, to contend with; but these young men and women,
or the greater part of them, have been born in the
Church, and brought up Latter-day Saints, and have
received the teachings that are necessary to advance
them in the kingdom of God on earth. If you are in any
way suspicious that the acts of your parents are not
right, if there is a conviction in your minds that they
feed appetites that are injurious to them, then it is for
you to abstain from that which you see is not good in
your parents.

Vol. II, 269-271, by Brigham Young, April 8, 1855:

causes of   There are many subjects upon which I wish to
disease   speak, but there is not time now, though in regard to
teachings pertaining to our temporal organization, I
will take the liberty of saying a few words. Do not some
of you have to send for doctors to draw your teeth, and
lie night after night with a bag of hot ashes, or hot salt,
on your faces, and say, "O dear, what a tooth ache I
children   have got?" When your children wake up in the night,
crying on account of a pain in their heads, do not some of
you go to the doctors, to see what they can do for the
little sufferers? Some of your children are afflicted with
humors in the head, and blotches upon the body, and
other ailments; and some of you have pains in various
parts of your bodies.

The fathers and mothers have laid the foundation
for many of these diseases, from generation to generation, until the people are reduced to their present
condition. True, some live to from fifty to ninety years

of age, but it is an unusual circumstance to see a man an hundred years old, or a woman ninety. The people have laid the foundation of short life through their diet, their rest, their labor, and their doing this, that, and the other in a wrong manner, with improper motives, and at improper times. I would be glad to instruct the people on these points, if they would hearken to me. I would be glad to tell mothers how to lay the foundation of health in their children, that they may be delivered from the diseases with which I am afflicted, and have been from my youth up.

Suppose I happen to say "Come, wife, let us have a good dinner today;" what does she get? Pork and beef boiled, stewed, roasted, and fried, potatoes, onions, cabbage, and turnips, custard, eggs, pies of all kinds, cheese, and sweet-meats. Now grant that I and my wife **overload** sit down and overload our stomachs, until we feel the **stomach** deleterious effects of it from the crowns of our heads to the soles of our feet, the whole system is disturbed in its operations, and is ready to receive and impart disease. A child begotten under such a condition of the systems of its parents, is liable to be born with a tabernacle subject to a life of pain and distress.

Will all the women hearken to this plain statement? No, you might as well talk to the wild geese that fly over us.

Again, a little hot tea, coffee, or sling, is generally given to a babe as soon as it comes into the world, to quiet the nerves, and make it sleep better; and I have seen my own wives almost whip their little ones to make them drink liquor. When I happen to see them, I say, "Stop that, that is something you may very well dispense with; do not put a drop of liquor into that child's mouth."

liquor   Some mothers, when bearing children, long for tea
tea   and coffee, or for brandy and other strong drinks, and if
coffee   they give way to that influence the next time they will want more, and the next still more, and thus lay the foundation for drunkenness in their offspring. An appetite is engendered, bred, and born in the child, and

it is a miracle if it does not grow up a confirmed drunkard.

Now will you, my sisters who are before me, hearken to good, sound common sense and reason? Will you commence now, and lay the foundation for a healthy posterity? Will you say, "I am determined not to desire this thing, or that, which will be injurious, but I will pray, and ask my Father in heaven for grace according to my day, that I may not desire that which will lay the foundation of ruin to my offspring, and to my posterity for generations? Or will you say, "Cannot I have a little tea, or a little whisky?"

The satisfying of these desires lays the foundation of sickness, disease, and short life. But if any one really desires a particular kind of food, or drink, and feels as though she could not do without it, let it be obtained, if possible; though it is far better to have faith to overcome such desires.

It is for us to stop the tide of physical degeneracy— to lay the foundation for a return to the position from which the human body has fallen. We have that privilege, by keeping ourselves pure. If we take the right course, our children will live longer than we shall, and their children will surpass their fathers, and have longer life, and so on, till they obtain to the age of those who lived in the early period of the world. The Prophet, speaking of the Saints in the last days, said, "For as the days of a tree are the days of my people, and mine elect shall long enjoy the work of their hands." Still, in the present short period of life some say that "this is a miserable world, I do not care how soon I get through." Well go and destroy yourselves, if you choose, you have all the opportunity that you can desire, there is plenty of arsenic, calomel, and other means, within your reach. But I would not give a cent for such persons; I do not delight in such characters, and I do not believe that the Lord delights in people who wish to die before they have accomplished the work that He designed for them to do. For a person to be willing to die is but a small part of the duties pertaining to the Gospel of salvation and the Gift of eternal life. We ought to prepare ourselves to live in the flesh, and overcome every sin, to live to the glory of God, to build up His kingdom, and to bring forth righteousness, salvation, and deliverance to the house of Israel, until the devil and his associates are driven from the earth, and he and his clan are bound and thrust down to hell, and a seal put upon them. Latter-day Saints who live merely to get ready to die are not worth much; rather get ready to live, and be prepared to live to the glory of your Father in heaven, and to do the work He has given you to do. That is our duty, and then we shall be ready to receive our blessings.

Vol. II, 357-359, by Ezra T. Benson, April 8, 1855:

I feel to rejoice this morning in the remarks that I have heard, and I feel to bear testimony to the same, and also to all the instructions given during this Conference.

I feel that it is good to be here, and I can say that I have tried to appreciate the blessings we enjoy in common with my brethren. It is indeed a privilege to rise before an assembly of Saints in the Valleys of the Mountains, before those that are now so comfortably and favorably located in this place; and while brother George A. Smith was speaking upon the "Word of Wisdom," there was a dream occurred to my mind that I heard related by one of the brethren a short time ago. He said there was a proclamation issued by the President of the Church of Jesus Christ, for the Elders of Israel to collect those together who had kept the commandments of God, for there was a work that the Lord had for them to perform. The people came together very slowly and reluctantly; once in a while a few would come along, but a leader off was wanted, and perhaps an Elder would be seen coming up, but it seemed to be slow work collecting the people together. After a while there was another proclamation issued for the people to come together in masses, those that were true, and that were known to be trying to keep the commandments of God, and they then came up by the thousands, by tens of thousands, and by hundreds of

dream

thousands. I felt that it was so this morning, that those who had been speaking had touched the right subject, and it was very good; and I felt that there would be very few in this vast congregation, (if they were called out,) who had kept the "Word of Wisdom;" if all such were called for, I am persuaded that there would be very few that would come forth, but if the word were, "Come forth, all ye Latter-day Saints that are trying to keep the Word of Wisdom," I feel that there would be many that would come forth, and I believe I would be among that number that would be found trying to keep the Word of Wisdom.

W. of W. more than tea, coffee, etc.

When we first heard the revelation upon the Word of Wisdom many of us thought it consisted merely in our drinking tea and coffee, but it is not only using tea and coffee and our tobacco and whisky, but it is every other evil which is calculated to contaminate this people. The Word of Wisdom implies to cease from adultery, to cease from all manner of excesses, and from all kinds of wickedness and abomination that are common amongst this generation—it is, strictly speaking, keeping the commandments of God, and living by every word that proceedeth from His mouth.

This is the way that I understand the Word of Wisdom, consequently we have to keep all the commandments, if I understand the matter correctly, in connexion with this Word of Wisdom, in order to obtain the blessings, for unless we do keep the commandments of God, and not offend in any one point, we have not a full claim upon the blessings promised in connexion with this portion of the word of the Lord.

The Lord says, in reference to these things mentioned in the Word of Wisdom, that they are not good for the body! I know that my brethren and sisters feel as I do, they have a desire to keep the Word of Wisdom, and know it is the wish of the Presidency that the Elders of Israel should preach upon the Word of Wisdom, and establish it in the minds of the people, and suffer not themselves from desire to be overcome by the habits of those among whom they travel to preach the Gospel, but be an example in all things.

I can say one thing which I am very thankful for, I never partook of an evil in my life because my brethren did, but I have always tried to act and live upon my own agency. If I have sinned, it has been through my own ignorance; if I go astray, it is because my mind and my nature are human.

I have ever felt determined to take a course to enjoy the Spirit of the Lord, and when He has left me to myself, and I have been tempted, I have always trusted in the Lord and endeavored to obey Him, and not to give way to the tempter; and I want this feeling to sink deep into the hearts of every man and woman calling themselves Latter-day Saints. And when I hear a word dropped by any one that will tend to thwart the design of God's holy word, why then I feel most indignant.

I wish to see men observe and teach the Word of Wisdom in their families, for to see men throw a bad influence upon the word of the Lord, I was going to say such a spirit is a stink in the nostrils of all righteous men.

Many of the Saints excuse themselves for chewing tobacco because others use it, but let us examine ourselves this morning, and see if such a course will be justifiable before our Heavenly Father.

Where is the man that excuses himself on this account? I ask him—is it righteousness for him to excuse himself in order to free himself from blame? If it is not, let him repent, cease his excusations, and turn unto the Lord his God, and work righteousness all the days of his life, that he may be saved in the kingdom of heaven.

Vol. II, 362-364, by George A. Smith, April 8, 1855:

If men wish to grow up in these mountains, free from disease, and from the power of the destroyer, and become strong and powerful like tigers—like giants in Israel, let them observe the principles laid down in the words of wisdom, let them observe them when they are children, let them grow up breathing a pure atmosphere, drinking pure water, and partaking of the wholesome vegetation, observing the words of wisdom, and they will grow up mighty men; one of them will be worth five dozen of those who are steeped and boiled by hot drinks, and tanned in tobacco juice.

Vol. III, 18-19, by Orson Pratt, May 20, 1855:

The spirit upon us should enable us to do that which is right, and that which is our duty. For instance, take the Word of Wisdom, which is given for our benefit and temporal salvation. It is true, disobedience to that is not so gross a sin as some others; but still, it is given for our temporal salvation, and should be observed. Now, it would require the servants of God to preach it every two weeks, or at least every month, to persuade this people to hearken to it; and yet they know it is the word of the Lord. If I were to call a vote, I presume that there would not be one that has come to the years of understanding but what would say, it is the word of God.

They go away, after hearing a most glorious discourse upon this and other revelations, and perhaps they will keep the Word of Wisdom two or three days; but it makes their head ache, and then they take a little tea, and it does them good for the moment, and they think the Lord don't know what they need as well as they do. I do not say that you do this, but your actions bespeak this. But it is such a trial! It must be a terrible trial, which the Lord said the weakest of all that are or can be called Saints could obey. A thing like tea to have influence over us, so that we can only obey the Word of Wisdom two days, and then break it, until we hear another discourse, and thus breaking our covenants, it shows the folly and weakness of man. It shows how the influence of one man prevails over another.

Why cannot you be independent beings, and say, "I will do this, and that, and the other, let my neighbor do as he may; let my neighbor do as he will, but as for me and my house, we will serve the Lord"? This is what ought to be.

In making these remarks I take them to myself, although I have, as an individual, been very strict in

temporal salvation

saying Lord doesn't know

relation to the Word of Wisdom since I have been in the Valley, and years before. Do not I like the good old tea? Yes I do, and when it is sweetened up, and a little cream turned in, it is very pleasant, as no doubt also was the forbidden fruit; but it is for me to use my endeavors to have it observed, by setting a good example, that I may have influence over my neighbor and over my family; and I do use that influence as far as is consistent, but it is difficult to persuade persons from their old habits.

destroy-
ing
angle

I wonder what those persons would do, if called to be martyred for their religion, who cannot do without violating the Word of Wisdom! I am aware that it is not constraint, and a man should not constrain his family to obey it, but every man will have to give an account of his doings, and abide the consequence, whatever it may be, if it be the destroying angel going through the land to slay the disobedient.

A man may keep the Word of Wisdom so far as tea, coffee, and tobacco are concerned, and still come very short. If he wishes and intends to be right, he must obey this, together with all the commandments and Words of Wisdom. We must regulate our thoughts, our comings in, our goings out, and all our doings and our minds by the Spirit of the Lord, and by the counsels of His servants. Can the destroyer have influence over such a man?

Let such a man stand up and say, "Lord, I have done as you told me, I have kept your words." Could such a man be destroyed before he had accomplished his work on the earth? I question it. Well, we shall undoubtedly see a time when we shall need such confidence as this.

Vol. III, 176-177, by Amasa Lyman, December 9, 1855:

more
than
tea and
coffee

Obey the Word of Wisdom. "Do you mean I shall not drink tea, or coffee?" I do not care whether you do or not. I do not consider that you obey the Word of Wisdom, simply, because you do not drink tea and coffee. May be you cannot get it. I have seen the time that I drank it when it was hard to get, and when I did not use it, when I could have got it.

Do not work yourselves to death, but try to live a long time, and learn to run and not weary, walk and not faint. Do you think of leaving off tea and coffee, alone, will enable you to scale the mountains, and outstrip the mountain goat in fleetness. It is just as true that weariness is the consequence of excessive toil as that God lives and reigns. It is manifest in you and me, and in every other part of His work. Keep the Word of Wisdom; and if you want to run and not weary, walk and not faint, call upon me and I will tell you how—just stop before you get tired.

The Word of Wisdom was given for a principle, with promise; as a rule of conduct, that should enable the people so to economize their time, and manage and control themselves, as not to eat and drink to excess, or use that which is hurtful to them; that they should be temperate in all things, in the exercise of labor, as well as in eating and drinking. Clothe yourselves properly if you can. Exercise properly if you can, and do right in everything.

<small>avoid excesses</small>

<small>exer-cise</small>

Do not stay the work of improvement and reform to pay attention to small things that are beneath your notice, but let it extend through the entire circle of your being, let it reach every relationship in life, and every avocation and duty embraced within your existence.

Let it affect your thinking, and the feelings which you cultivate, and let there be nothing pertaining to your being but what shall be influenced by it. The Word of Wisdom would itself save you, if you would only keep it, in the true sense and spirit of it, comprehending the purpose for which it was given.

<small>W. of W. can save</small>

It reaches everything that affects your happiness. Go on then and observe the Word of Wisdom. What does wisdom tell you? Let tea and coffee alone, and abstain from that which would overtax the strength of your system, and favor the innovations of disease, and shorten your lives, and thereby limit the extent of your usefulness.

Study to save yourselves. That which saves your life, and lengthens out your days is salvation. And that which fills out your days with the perpetration of good is salvation—it helps to make up the sum of your salvation.

I want you to look at it in this point of view, and be influenced by the spirit of truth, foster it within the fountains of your feelings, and it will give a good character to your conduct.

This will be living your religion every day, in every thing you do; you will have nothing to do outside of your religion.

Now that you may have wisdom to adopt this course of life, and live to enjoy the blessings that will accrue from its adoption, is my prayer in the name of Jesus Christ. Amen.

Vol. VII, 352-354, by Erastus Snow, January 5, 1860:

Our Father in heaven ... seeks ... to secure to intelligent beings the boon they most earnestly desire— namely, the continuation of lives....

desire
to live

Why is this universal desire planted in the human breast to live? It is a law ordained in nature for good. We may call it instinct, or by what name we please—it is a universal law in all intelligent beings to seek to retain the organization they possess. Hence when sickness assails us, an enemy appears in deadly array with a show to lay us low in death; every faculty of the soul is aroused to repel it, and we use all the means in our power to stay the progress of disease.

The Scriptures inform us that the greatest gift of God is eternal life. Is this a gift of God in deed and in truth? Yes; I understand it to be, to all intents and purposes, the gift of God. Yet eternal life is not attained without compliance on our part with those principles that lead to the attainment of it. I will illustrate this by what we see daily in our natural life. We understand, by what we learn daily, that there are certain things that tend to destroy this tabernacle; and there are other things which, if we deserve, have a tendency to prolong the organization of this tabernacle and our temporal existence.

natural
laws

For example, we have learned, by numerous observations and examples, that if an individual cast himself into the sea, without having any means of floating, he will sink in the water and under it, and he cannot live. A certain thing is necessary to his existence, which is the pure, wholesome air inhaled into the lungs. Anything that cuts us off from this supply terminates our earthly existence: the machinery of this tabernacle cannot be kept in motion without it. We have also learned that excessive heat or excessive cold will stop this machinery of life in our mortal tabernacles. If we would prolong our organization for any certain number of years, we must carefully guard against those evils that endanger our tabernacles. Excesses of every kind have a tendency to weaken, and ultimately to destroy the tabernacle of man. An excessive appetite, if encouraged with rich viands, and this persisted in, will make the possessor a glutton, and shorten his mortal career.

over-
stimulate
nervous
system

If a person having a strong desire for stimulants, such as spiritous liquors, tea, coffee, tobacco, opium, &c, that stimulate the nervous system to excess, and continues to gratify this appetite, will soon destroy the elasticity of his nervous system, and become like a bow that is often bent almost to breaking. If a bow be kept strung up to its utmost tension, it loses its power and strength, until it is of little or no use.

avoid
excesses

excesses
tax
nervous
system

So in nature: the more any powerful stimulant is made use of in the human system, the sooner the human machinery will be worn out. It follows, then, if we will secure life and preserve the organization of this tabernacle, we must observe the laws of life—we must abstain from intemperance of every description. We must neither indulge in excessive eating, excessive drinking, nor in excessive working, whereby to overtax our physical energies or our nervous system. Perhaps no kind of labor will so rapidly weaken the power of life within us, or strength of these tabernacles, like excessive mental labour, because it has a more direct influence upon the nervous system. The nervous system seems to be a sort of connecting link between our spirit and our tabernacles. Yet a proper amount of labour, physical and mental, becomes necessary to the proper development of the faculties of both body and soul.

The child that has never faith to attempt to walk, as a matter of course, will never learn to walk. When he first begins to exercise his feet and legs to walk, they are weak, and scarcely capable of supporting his little frame; but the more he exercises them, the more he receives strength. And so with every other portion of the tabernacle. The same may be said of all mental gifts and endowments. The mind that is naturally stupid, dull, and inactive, and no outward circumstances are brought to bear upon it, to impel it to exercise—that mind remains comparatively undeveloped; that spirit does not improve, not increase in strength and capacity.

mental
exer-
cise

The more the mental faculties are brought into exercise, if it is not immoderate exercise, the more these faculties receive strength, and the greater powers of research are developed in that spirit; and where shall the end thereof be?

unlim-
ited
mental
abili-
ties

There is no end to its increase of knowledge and truth, unless we turn round and go the other way; in other words, unless we persistently pursue the path of death and violate every law, both physical and mental, until we become dissolved.

down-
ward
spiral

If we cease temperate habits, and give ourselves up to the gratification of our lusts and appetites, and pursue this course from year to year, we shall find ourselves steadily going down to the chambers of death, and no power can hinder it: it is a fixed law of our physical existence. Can the Lord change it? I will not stop to inquire whether he can or not. I will say, however, I never heard of his doing it on any other condition than that individual repenting of his evil course. When he does this, and observes the laws of life and health, God will add his blessing to his efforts, and he will begin to ascend the hill again, and he may regain in some measure that which he has lost. But as long as he continues that course of evil, no power can redeem him.

Vol. VIII, 57-58, by Brigham Young, May 20, 1860:

You do not see me here every Sabbath. Perhaps
some of you wonder why. I will tell you in a very few
words. If I had my own choice, and could have my own
dictation with regard to physical and mental labour, I
would set apart, for the express benefit of man, at least
one-seventh part of time for rest. There are but very few
Sabbaths that I have ever kept in strictly resting from
my labours—permitting both body and mind to rest.
Perhaps assembling here on the Sabbath is a rest to
many, though it is not very much of a rest. To those who
have been labouring all the week to the utmost extent of
their strength, it may be somewhat of a rest to sit on
these hard benches; but when I come here I have a
constant labour on my mind. This congregation, the
Saints throughout the world, and the world of mankind
in general are before me. I think for them all. I would
like to take one-seventh part of the time to rest; but I do
not often have this privilege. If I had my own mind, I
would devote the time for meetings like this within the
measure of the six days, and on the seventh, rest from
all my labours, for the express purpose of renewing the
mental and physical powers of man. They require it, as
the Lord well knew; hence he established a day of rest.
The natural tendency of the physical powers of man is to
decay; and to preserve them as long as possible, they
need this retirement from labour—this rest—this ease.
I very seldom enjoy this privilege.

Our customs are more or less like the customs of
our fathers, and their influence is often stronger upon us
than any law. There is not a law of God, nor a law of any
nation that exercises so strong an influence upon us as
do our traditions at times, to bind us to certain customs,
habits, and ceremonies: consequently, to carry out the
old traditions, we observe this day of rest as we now do.
Father went to meeting on the seventh day, and the
priests and all good people go to meeting on that day. It
has been the custom from time immemorial. Some men
and women walk miles to attend meetings; some men
walk as many as ten miles, hold two or three meetings,
walk back, and are in their workshops by five o'clock on

[margin: Sabbath rest needed]

[margin: effect of tradition]

Monday morning. Custom binds us to this, and here we are today in compliance with its force.

Vol. VIII, 60-61, by Brigham Young, May 20, 1860:

Isaiah's prophecy of millennium

You read in the Bible, "There shall be no more thence an infant of days, nor an old man that hath not filled his days; for the child shall die an hundred years old; but the sinner, being an hundred years old, shall be accursed. And they shall build houses and inhabit them; and they shall plant vineyards, and eat the fruit of them. They shall not build and another inhabit; they shall not plant and another eat; for as the days of a tree are the days of my people, and mine elect shall long enjoy the work of their hands. They shall not labour in vain, nor bring forth for trouble; for they are the seed of the blessed of the Lord, and their offspring with them."

mankind degenerated

The human family has again to return to this state—not you and I as individuals. Mankind have degenerated; they have lost the physical and mental power they once possessed.

Vol. VIII, 63-64, by Brigham Young, May 20, 1860:

fruit

vegetables

If the days of man are to begin to return, we must cease all extravagant living. When men live to the age of a tree, their food will be fruit. Mothers, to produce offspring full of life and days, must cease drinking liquor, tea, and coffee, that their systems may be free from bad effects. If every woman in this Church will now cease drinking tea, coffee, liquor, and all other powerful stimulants, and live upon vegetables, &c, not many generations will pass away before the days of man will again return. But it will take generations to entirely eradicate the influence of deleterious substances. This must be done before we can attain our paradisaical state, for the Lord will bring again Zion to its paradisaical state.

May God grant that we may see and enjoy it. Amen.

Vol. VIII, 138-139, 140, by Brigham Young, August 5, 1860:

Our spirits were pure and holy when they entered our tabernacles; and if they have been defiled, it has been by the influence of Satan, through the weakness of the flesh. There is a constant warfare, and in the great majority of cases the flesh overcomes the spirit. In the few cases where the spirit overcomes the flesh, it yields obedience to the whisperings of the eternal Spirit of truth, which elevates it above the power of all unholy desires and passiones.

influence of Satan

Is there anything on this earth you could not dispense with, for the sake of the Gospel? There should not be.

Our bodies are organized to derive enjoyment from their proper use. There is enjoyment in eating when you are hungry, and in resting when you are fatigued, to the extent the body rightly requires; but if appetite is so gratified that your body, when you wake, is tormented with a raging fever, where is the pleasure in eating so much of this or that delicious food? Satisfying the brings to an end the pleasure of eating; and where food is partaken chiefly to gratify the pleasurable sensation derived from eating, disease is gendered and true misery springs out of this unwise gratification. Some healthy, strong-constitutioned persons can eat large quantities of food with apparent impunity; but, in so doing, the tax they place upon their systems will ultimately bring disease and death.

appe-
tite
brings
disease

Those who have suffered excessive thirst while passing over plains and deserts realize that there is no blessing that is greater than cold water. When the system is thus parched for want of the proper supply of moisture to sustain the continual perspiration it is subject to, is there any luxury on the earth that can excell pure, cold water? Though, in case of excessive thirst and consequent exhaustion, care is required not to drink too freely, until the system is cooled, and becomes gradually imbued with this life-restoring element. But through the use of water, by-and-by your

water

thirst comes to an end, and you feel as though you had not been thirsty in your lives: the enjoyment has passed away.

Shall we try to cultivate our minds, our feelings, the talent God has given us, so that we may improve continually and grow in grace and in the knowledge of the truth, and cultivate wisdom in ourselves, and so live that we can truthfully say, to-day, that we are masters over every appetite? The person that wants the whisky, cannot you do without it? Which would you part with first—your tobacco, your whisky, or your religion?

tobacco
whisky
or
religion

Vol. IX, 35-36, by Brigham Young, April 7, 1861:

A doctor told an old lady in New York, when she insisted upon his telling her whether snuff would injure her brain, "It will not hurt the brain of anyone, for no person that has brains will take snuff." I will say that the most filthy way of using tobacco is to smoke it. "What is the neat way? If you are going to direct any course for the people to use tobacco, let us know what it is. Cannot you who have used it for years point out a neat, modest, judicious way of using it?" The "Word of Wisdom" says that tobacco is good for sick cattle; and when you want another chew, down with it as you would a pill. It may make you vomit a little, but that is soon over, and it is good for sick cattle. That is the neatest way you can use tobacco.

ways to
use
tobacco

Vol. IX, 184, by Daniel H. Wells, September 29, 1861:

...It is our business, and duty, too, to take care of all that the Lord has put into our hands, and not because a word has been said about tea, to go and burn it up or throw it away; but we should put all we are made stewards over to the best possible use.

Now, I have no objection to our keeping things in our possession that are necessary for sickness, but let whisky and the tobacco be put to their legitimate uses, then all will be right. Where coffee is produced, the people do not use it, but they raise it for the barbarians. In the East Indies and wherever coffee is grown, the

coffee
growers'
attitude

physi-
cians

inhabitants consider it poison and wonder that it does not poison the outside barbarians, as they term all those whom we consider the civilized and enlightened nations. Some of our physicians will, however, say and contend that it is perfectly harmless, when the facts before us show the effect of coffee, tea, opium, tobacco and other stimulants, and various other foolish and expensive indulgencies to be the cause of reducing the average of human life, so that not one half of those born into the world to attain the age of seventeen years.

Vol. XI, 132, by Brigham Young, August 1-10, 1865:

lay
founda-
tion
of
health

Prepare to die, is not the exhortation in this church and kingdom; but prepare to live is the word with us, and improve all we can in this life that we may be the better prepared to enjoy a better life hereafter, wherein we may enjoy a more exalted condition of intelligence, wisdom, light, knowledge, power, glory, and exaltation. Then let us seek to extend the present life to the uttermost, by observing every law of health, and by properly balancing labor, study, rest, and recreation, and thus prepare for a better life. Let us teach these principles to our children, that, in the morning of their days, they may be taught to lay the foundation of health and strength and constitution and power of life in their bodies.

Vol. XI, 366, 367, by E. T. Benson, April 7, 1867:

...the "point" is "to be one" in everything that pertains to the building up of the Kingdom of God. And if we are to believe what we have heard during this Conference it is to be one in keeping the Word of Wisdom, and in living by every word that proceeds from the mouth of the Almighty through His servants. It is true that we have heard this for years, and it will have to be sounded in our ears until we are one in Christ as He is one with the Father.

eat
drink
and wear

We have been taught during this Conference to dispense with everything in eating, drinking, and wearing that is not in accordance with the will of God....

We all know that there are a great many things that we now eat, drink, and wear, with which we could dispense to our own advantage, but ... there is no peace until all these wants are supplied.

Talking about happiness, I told a lady to-day at noon that we, generally, are very ignorant of it. We think that a good bonnet, hat, a fine coat, a good cup of tea, or a pipe of tobacco ... will make us happy, but it is a mistaken notion.... We can be happy only in keeping the commandments of God and in being wholly devoted to the things of His kingdom.

to
please
Lord

God ... has borne with us these many years; but, if I can discern the signs of the times, He is now going to require these things at our hands. Supposing He had given the Word of Wisdom as a command, how many of us would have been here? I do not know; but He gave this without command or restraint, observing that it would be pleasing in His sight for His people to obey its precepts. Ought we not to try to please our Heavenly Father ... ?

Vol. XII, 36-37, by Brigham Young, April 14, 1867:

sweets
and
over-
eating

In foreign lands you may find districts where many of the people do not have, probably, more than two-thirds of what they need to eat—and they live thus from year to year—yet you will find them much more healthy than they who gorge themselves continually. Take the Americans, say in the old Granite Stake where I have travelled, and to look at their surroundings out of doors you would not think they had more than one bean to a pint of water, but go into their houses and you will find beef, pork, apple pie, custard pie, pumpkin pie, mince pie, and every luxury, and they live so as to shorten their days and the days of their children. You may think that these things are not of much importance; no more they are, unless they are observed, but let the people observe them and they lay the foundation for longevity, and they will begin to live out their days, not only a hundred years, but, by and bye, hundreds of years on the earth. Do you think they will stuff themselves then

with tea and coffee, and perhaps with a little brandy
sling before breakfast and a little before going to bed,
and then beef, pork, mutton, sweet-meats, and pastry,
morning, noon, and night? No; you will find they will
live as our first parents did, on fruits and on a little
simple food, and they will never overload the stomach.

Let the people be temperate in their food ...

Vol. XII, 44-45, by George Q. Cannon, April 21, 1867:

... I do not like to hear anybody express himself as
though this movement in relation to keeping the Word of
Wisdom is one got up and sustained only by enthusiasm.
I do not call that enthusiasm which prompts people to
walk up to the line of their duty and renounce evil
practices, and when I hear men say—"I have seen the
people get enthusiastic about the Word of Wisdom
before, but they have soon relapsed into their old
habits," I consider it wrong. We ought not to require to
be talked to and counselled on points so well recognised
and established as this. God has given to us a most
positive promise on this subject, and we should be
diligent in carrying it into effect without waiting to be
counselled, getting up an excitement, or acting on the
spur of the moment, and after awhile returning to old
habits. I do not think any person will be benefitted by
acting in this manner. There should be a well settled
conviction in the mind of every person belonging to this
Church that it would be a real benefit for him or her to
observe the Word of Wisdom, and to carry into effect the
counsel God has given on any point. If I do not see the
evils that result from smoking and chewing tobacco,
drinking liquor, tea, and coffee, or eating meats to
excess, and the benefits that would result from
abstaining, what anybody else may see would only have
a temporary effect upon me. I must feel in my own heart
that it is injurious to me to indulge in these things, there
must be a well settled conviction within me that this is
the case, then when I am thrown in contact with persons
who use them, and inducements are offered me to do the
same, it is easy for me to decline, because I am satisfied

enthusi-
astic
spurts
of
obedi-
ence
to
W. of W.

in my own mind that they are injurious, and there is no need of excitement or enthusiasm to enable me to refrain.

Our teachings during Conference will, at any rate, induce parents and guardians to keep their children from learning pernicious habits, which in early life are so easily acquired, and which when acquired retain their hold upon us with such tenacity, and if, in addition to this, five hundred people throughout the Territory are induced to keep the Word of Wisdom I do not think that our preaching will have been in vain. But I anticipate far greater results than this. It is true, probably, that there are many points concerning our welfare that may not have been touched upon by our Heavenly Father in the Word of Wisdom, but in my experience I have noticed that they who practice what the Lord has already given are keenly alive to other words of wisdom and counsel that may be given. I would consider that for a person who was in a profuse perspiration to go into the wind without being properly clothed would be more foolish and injurious than to eat meat or to drink tea or coffee to excess. There are a thousand ways in which we can act unwisely; our attention has been directed to some few points, and if we observe them the Lord has promised us great treasures of wisdom, which will enable us to see a thousand points where we can take better care of our bodies, preserve our health, and which will enable us to train our children in the way of the Lord. The result will be that our children will be healthy and strong, and we will raise up a generation that will be a blessing to us, and through whom the Lord can accomplish His great and mighty works in the earth.

Vol. XII, 117-119, 122, by Brigham Young, August 17, 1867:

free
agency

We can enjoy the blessings of heaven, or we can deprive ourselves of that enjoyment. Intelligent beings have the power to exercise their free will and choice in doing good, equally as much as in doing evil. All have the privilege of doing evil if they are disposed so to do,

but they will always find that the wages of sin is death.
The Latter-day Saints, by their righteousness, can
enjoy all the blessings which the Lord has promised to
bestow upon His people, and they can, by their
unrighteousness, deprive themselves of the enjoyment
of those blessings. We, for instance, exhort the Saints to
observe the Word of Wisdom, that they may, through its
observance, enjoy the promised blessing. Many try to
excuse themselves because tea and coffee are not
mentioned, arguing that it refers to hot drinks only.
What did we drink hot when that Word of Wisdom was
given? Tea and coffee. It definitely refers to that which
we drink with our food. I said to the Saints at our last
annual Conference, the Spirit whispers to me to call
upon the Latter-day Saints to observe the Word of
Wisdom, to let tea, coffee, and tobacco alone, and to
abstain from drinking spiritous drinks. This is what the
Spirit signifies through me. If the Spirit of God whispers
this to His people through their leader, and they will not
listen nor obey, what will be the consequence of their
disobedience? Darkness and blindness of mind with
regard to the things of God will be their lot; they will
cease to have the spirit of prayer, and the spirit of the
world will increase in them in proportion to their
disobedience until they apostatize entirely from God
and His ways.

This is no new or strange thing that you are
required to do. Thirty-five years ago we were called
upon to reform in our lives, by giving heed to the same
Words of Wisdom; and if any man comes to you and tells
you that you must have a little tea and a little coffee, by
the same rule he may urge you to take a little tobacco
and a little intoxicating liquor, or a little of any other
substance which is hurtful to man. This destroys their
claim and right to the spirit of revelation, and they go
into darkness. There is not a single Saint deprived of the
privilege of asking the Father, in the name of Jesus
Christ, our Savior, if it is true that the Spirit of the
Almighty whispers through His servant Brigham to
urge upon the Latter-day Saints to observe the Word of
Wisdom.

(margin notes: hot drinks tea and coffee; 35 years)

If you observe faithfully the Word of Wisdom, you will have your dollar, your five dollars, your hundred dollars, yea, you will have your hundreds of dollars to spend for that which will be useful and profitable to you.

perni-
cious
habits
sap
founda-
tion

Why should we continue to practise in our lives those pernicious habits that have already sapped the foundation of the human constitution, and shortened the life of man to that degree that a generation passes away in the brief period of from twenty-seven to twenty-nine years? The strength, power, beauty and glory that once adorned the form and constitution of man have vanished away before the blighting influences of inordinate appetite and love of this world. Doubtless we are about the best looking people to-day upon this footstool, and about the healthiest; but where is the iron constitution, the marrow in the bone, the power in the loins, and the strength in the sinew and muscle of which the ancient fathers could boast? These have, in great measure, passed away; they have decayed from generation to generation, until constitutional weakness and effeminacy are bequeathed to us through the irregularities and sins of our fathers. The health and power and beauty that once adorned the noble form of man must again be restored to our race; and God designs that we shall engage in this great work of restoration. Then let us not trifle with our mission, by indulging in the use of injurious substances. These lay the foundation of disease and death in the systems of men, and the same are committed to their children, and another generation of feeble human beings is introduced into the world. Such children have insufficient bone, sinew, muscle, and constitution, and are of little use to themselves, or to their fellow creatures; they are

900
years

not prepared for life, but for the grave; not to live five, six, eight, and nine hundred years, but to appear for a moment, as it were, and pass away. Now, when a person is fifty years of age he or she is considered an old man or an old woman; they begin to feel decrepit, and think they must feel old, appear old, and begin to die. Premature death is in the marrow of their bones, the seeds of early dissolution are sown in their bodies, they feel old at fifty, sixty, and seventy years, when they should feel like boys of fifteen, sixteen, and seventeen. Instead of feeling decrepit at those years they should feel full of strength, vigor, and life, having attained to early maturity, prepared now to enter upon the duties of a long future life, and when two hundred years have been attained, they should then feel more vigorous than the healthiest of men do in this age at forty and fifty years.

Instead of doing two days' work in one day, wisdom would dictate to our sisters, and to every other person, that if they desire long life and good health, they must, after sufficient exertion, allow the body to rest before it is entirely exhausted. When exhausted, some argue that they need stimulants in the shape of tea, coffee, spiritous liquors, tobacco, or some of those narcotic substances which are often taken to goad on the lagging powers to greater exertions, but instead of these kind of stimulants they should recruit by rest. Our artificial wants, and not our real wants, and the ofllowing of senseless customs subject our sisters to an excess of labor. To supply these wants—to get a ribbon, an artificial flower, this, that, and the other gew-gaw, rather than substantial necessaries—our farmers sell their wheat. Work less, wear less, eat less, and we shall be a great deal wiser, healthier, and wealthier people than by taking the course we now do. This whole Yankee nation eat so much, and so many good things, that they are always poor in their bodily habit; now and then only you will see a fleshy person among them; it is also the case with the people of the southern portion of the nation. It is difficult to find anything more healthy to drink than good cold water, such as flows down to us from springs and snows of our mountains. This is the beverage we should drink. It should be our drink at all times. If we constantly drink even malt liquor made from our barley and wheat, our health would be injured more or less thereby. It may be remarked that some men who use spiritous liquors and tobacco are healthy, but I argue that they would be much more healthy if they did not use it, and then they are entitled to the

rest
needed

pure
water

blessings promised to those who observe the advice given in the "Word of Wisdom." Some few persons who have been addicted to the use of hot drinks, &c., have reached the age of eighty, eighty-three, and eighty-four years, but had they not been addicted to such habits of living they might have reached the age of a hundred or a hundred and five years.

Vol. XII, 156, by Brigham Young, January 12, 1868:

will
of
God

To observe the Word of Wisdom is nothing more than we ought to have done over thirty years ago. Touching this matter, I tell the people the will of God concerning them, and then they are left to do as they please in obeying it or not. It is a piece of good counsel which the Lord desires His people to observe, that they may live on the earth until the measure of their creation is full. This is the object the Lord had in view in giving that Word of Wisdom. To those who observe it He will give great wisdom and understanding, increasing their health, giving strength and endurance to the faculties of their bodies and minds until they shall be full of years upon the earth. This will be their blessing if they will observe His word with a good and willing heart and in faithfulness before the Lord.

Vol. XII, 158, by Brigham Young, February 8, 1868:

how
and
when
W. of W.
received

...The prophet began to instruct them how to live that they might be the better prepared to perform the great work they were called to accomplish. I think I am as well acquainted with the circumstances which led to the giving of the Word of Wisdom as any man in the Church, although I was not present at the time to witness them. The first school of the prophets was held in a small room situated over the Prophet Joseph's kitchen, in a house which belonged to Bishop Whitney, and which was attached to his store, which store probably might be about fifteen feet square. In the rear of this building was a kitchen, probably ten by fourteen feet, containing rooms and pantries. Over this kitchen was situated the room in which the Prophet received revelations and in which he instructed his brethren. The brethren came to that place for hundreds of miles to attend school in a little room probably no larger than eleven by fourteen. When they assembled together in this room after breakfast, the first thing they did was to light their pipes, and, while smoking, talk about the great things of the kingdom, and spit all over the room, and as soon as the pipe was out of their mouths a large chew of tobacco would then be taken. Often when the Prophet entered the room to give the school instructions he would find himself in a cloud of tobacco smoke. This, and the complaints of his wife at having to clean so filthy a floor, made the Prophet think upon the matter, and he inquired of the Lord relating to the conduct of the Elders in using tobacco, and the revelation known as the Word of Wisdom was the result of his inquiry. You know what it is, and can read it at your leisure.

So we see that almost the very first teachings of the first Elders of this Church received were as to what to eat, what to drink, and how to order their natural lives, that they might be united temporally as well as spiritually.

Vol. XII, 176, by Erastus Snow, October 8, 1867:

I am persuaded that the subject last referred to by President Young—the prolongation of life and the preservation of health cannot be over-rated. This is one of the subjects relating to our temporal welfare that received the early attention of the Prophet Joseph, and the revelation commonly called the Word of Wisdom has been before the people for over thirty years. I feel assured that a word on this subject kindly spoken by our President is a prompting from on high, and I believe that every true Elder in Israel will bear witness that this is the word of the Lord to us at this time. I exhort teach every Bishop and presiding Elder in this city as well as others throughout the country to lay this matter to heart as one W. of W. subject requiring their special attention. Not to make it a hobby to the exclusion of everything else, so as to disgust the people, but in the true spirit of the Gospel seek to bring this matter home to the hearts and understandings of the people of their respective wards and settlements. Feel after those who may be stupid and ignorant, who do not come to meeting, and do not receive the spirit of this Conference. Let the Bishops and others in authority endeavor through their teachers and otherwise to search out such individuals, and dig round about them, and prune them that they may perchance bring forth fruit.

Vol. XII, 192-193, by Brigham Young, April 6, 1868:

The items of instruction which have been laid before us by Elders George A. Smith and George Q. Cannon are very important to us, they are subjects which we have dwelt upon for years. It is generally known among us that we commenced some years ago to raise cotton in the southern portion of our Territory, and it is also known that machinery to manufacture it has been introduced into this country. All this has been done to encourage the people to become self-sustaining. I am ready to acknowledge that the Latter-day Saints are the best people, and the most willing people to do right that I know anything about. But when we take into particular and close consideration their acts, and compare them with the teaching they are constantly receiving, we think and say they are very far from taking all the counsel given them of the Lord through His servants. But were they to be counseled, for instance, to go to the gold mines, many of them would obey with alacrity. If they were to be counseled to chew or smoke tobacco, many would lift up both hands for this, and shout for joy? If the sisters many of them, were counseled to continue the use of tea and coffee they would sit up all night to bless you. When we are counseled to do that which pleases us then are we willing to obey counsel. Yet when I consider the pit from whence we have been taken, and the rock from whence we have been hewn, I can say, praise to the Latter-day Saints. Again, when we consider the immensity of knowledge and wisdom and understanding pertaining to the things of this life, pertaining to the learning of this world, pertaining to that which is within our reach, and ready for the use and profit of the people, and particularly with regard to

obey
what
pleases
us

taking care of ourselves, and then consider our shortcomings, and slothfulness, we may look upon ourselves with shame-facedness because of the smallness of our attainments in the midst of so many great advantages.

refor-
mation
needed
in
food
and
drink

swine
flesh

A thorough reformation is needed in regard to our eating and drinking, and on this point I will freely express myself, and shall be glad if the people will hear, believe and obey. If the people were willing to receive the true knowledge from heaven in regard to their diet they would cease eating swine's flesh. I know this as well as Moses knew it, and without putting it in a code of commandments. When I tell you that it is the will of the Lord to cease eating swine's flesh, very likely some one will tell you that it is the will of the Lord to stop eating beef and mutton, and another that it is the will of the Lord to stop eating fowl and fish until the minds of the people become bewildered, so that they know not how to decide between right and wrong, truth and error. The beef fed upon our mountain grasses is as healthy food as we need at present. Beef, so fattened, is as good as wild meat, and is quite different in its nature from stall-fed meat. But we can eat fish; and I ask the people of this community, who hinders you from raising fowls for their eggs? Who hinders you from cultivating fruit of every variety that will flourish in the different parts of this Territory? There has not been a day through the whole winter that I have not had fresh peaches, and plenty of apples and strawberries. Who hinders any person in this community from having these different kinds of food in their families? Fish is as healthy a food as we can eat, if we except vegetables and fruit, and with them will become a very wholesome diet. What hinders us from surrounding ourselves with an abundance of these various articles of food which will promote health and produce longevity? If it is anything, it is our own neglect; or, in other words, which will answer my purpose better, the want of knowing how.

Vol. XII, 198-199, by George A. Smith, April 6, 1868:

meat

swine
flesh

There is another subject under consideration, which weighs very heavily upon the minds of the Saints. The Word of Wisdom recommends us to use the flesh of animals sparingly. The law of Moses prohibited to Israel the use of swine's flesh; but in the Gentile world at the present day it is considered superior, as food, to amost every other kind of flesh. And even among us, with the education and training that we have received, there is a great deal of it used. It seems to be a pretty general idea among the people that swine's flesh can be more easily raised than any other; but there is no doubt that, with proper care and attention, other kinds of meat might be produced with equal facility. For some reason God, by special law, prohibited its use to the children of Israel; and it certainly seems desirable that we should also discontinue its use, as within the past few years in some countries where a great amount of pork has been consumed the people have been afflicted with a kind of pestilence—a disease which is considered incurable. It is therefore wise and prudent for us to adopt plans to procure supplies from other sources. In some countries the culture of fish has recently been introduced. It was commenced, in the first place, by sportsmen for the purpose of increasing the amusement of anglers; but the French government, under the reign of the present Emperor, have commenced to stock the rivers of France with fish for the purpose of increasing the supply of healthful food to the people. This is being done successfully in New England, where the rivers were formerly well stocked with salmon and other varieties of fish, though for many years they have become extinct. Laws have been passed in New Hampshire, Maine and other Eastern States, requiring the owners of mills to construct fishways over their dams, so that fish can pass freely up and down the streams, the dams having heretofore effectually prevented this.

Persons have also been employed to re-stock the rivers, and in this way many choice varieties of fish have been again successfully introduced. The real fact is, they are as easily raised as hogs, if the proper attention is paid to them. Our beautiful lakes—such as Utah Lake and Bear Lake—our rivers, and even our springs can, with a very little trouble and expense, be made to yield an immense quantity of this healthful food. I wish to call the attention of the Bishops and Elders, at home and abroad, to the propriety of studying this question; and if they lack information on the subject just let them drop a note to the Hon. W. H. Hooper, our Delegate at Washington, and ask him to furnish information on the culture of fish. He has it in his reach through the Bureau of Agriculture, and can send it under his own frank, and that will put you in possession of the information you require. You can feed fish as well as hogs, and they will eat a great many things you are little aware of, and with a little trouble you can procure that which will furnish an agreeable and healthy change in our diet.

poul-
try

I also wish to advise our brethren—the Bishops especially, to consider the propriety of taking proper measures for the production of poultry. Their flesh is agreeable and much more healthful as food than using great quantities of pork, as we are compelled to do in many instances.

Vol. XII, 201-202, 203, 204, by Brigham Young, April 8, 1868:

chil-
dren

good
food
for
chil-
dren

...I would like to see the time when our sisters will take more pains to beautify their children. When your children arise in the morning instead of sending them out of doors to wash in cold, hard water, with a little soft soap, and wiping them as though you would tear the skin off them, creating roughness and darkness of skin, take a piece of soft flannel, and wipe the faces of your children smooth and nice, dry them with a soft cloth; and instead of giving them pork for their breakfast, give them good wholesome bread and sweet milk, baked potatoes, and also buttermilk if they like it, and a little fruit, and I would have no objections to their eating a little rice. Rice is an excellent food for children, and I wish some of the brethren would cultivate it in these valleys. Upland rice will flourish in this country. Train up your children to be beautiful and fair, instead of neglecting them until they are sunburned and become like the natives of our mountains. Let the sisters take care of themselves, and make themselves beautiful, and if any of you are so superstitious and ignorant as to say that this is pride, I can say that you are not informed as to the pride which is sinful before the Lord, you are also ignorant as to the excellency of the heavens, and of

beauty the beauty which dwells in the society of the Gods. Were you to see an angel, you would see a beautiful and lovely creature. Make yourselves like angels in goodness and beauty. Let the mothers in Israel make their sons and daughters healthy and beautiful, by cleanliness and a proper diet. Whether you have much or little clothing for your children, it can be kept clean and healthy, and be made to fit their persons neatly. Make your children lovely and fair that you may delight in them. Cease to send out your children to herd sheep with their skins exposed to the hot sun, until their hands and faces appear as though they lived in an ash heap.

...I would just as soon see you wear hats with wide

fashion brims as not, if you have that fashion that will give
and comfort and convenience and produce health and
health longevity. We wish to promote the longevity of the people. Tell your husbands to get you a heifer calf or two and some chickens, and you will feed them, and take care of them, instead of feeding pigs, and if your

fish, husbands have springs on their land, get them to clean
poul- them out and dam them up a little, and introduce the
try; spawn of the best fish we have in these mountains, and
not collect all the information that has been printed, and
pigs which comes within your reach on the subject of raising fish. And raise your potatoes and parsnips and carrots for feeding them with, adding a little corn meal, or a little oat meal. We can raise fish here, and the cost will

chick- be one fourth less per pound than other meats. You may
ens think that fowls are injurious to the garden; but they are
and not. They will pick up grubs and cut worms and other
gar destructive insects, and the good they do in this respect
dens will far overbalance any trifling injury they may do to

young plants. They will keep your gardens clean of these pests, and fatten, giving you plenty of eggs to eat. Take care of them, and get a little patch of lucerne planted to give to your young heifer, and rear her until she gives you increase.

storage

...Sisters, do not ask your husbands to sell the last bushel of grain you have to buy something for you out of the stores, but aid your husbands in storing it up against a day of want, and always have a year or two's provision on hand. A great abundance of fruit can be dried. There are but few families in this city who do not have the privilege of drying and laying up fruit. Yet the majority of families in this community, instead of using fruit that was dried last fall but one, are using fruit dried last year when the grasshoppers were here. A year's supply should be kept ahead, so that families would not be compelled to eat fruit that had been injured by grasshoppers and other insects. We should accumulate all kinds of nutritive substances, and preserve them from worms, which can easily be done. If we do not take care of ourselves, we shall have a very poor chance to be taken care of.

Vol. XII, 221-224, by George Q. Cannon, April 7, 1868:

We have heard considerable of late, especially since twelve months today, on the subject of the Word of Wisdom. Almost every elder who has spoken from this stand has felt the necessity and importance of calling the attention of the people to this subject. We are told, and very plainly, too, that hot drinks—tea, coffee, chocolate, cocoa and all drinks of this kind—are not good for man. We are also told that alcoholic drinks are not good, and that tobacco when either smoked or chewed is an evil. We are told that swine's flesh is not good, and that we should dispense with it; and we are told that flesh of any kind is not suitable to man in the summer time, and ought to be eaten sparingly in the winter. The question arises in the minds of a great many people, "What then are we to eat if we drop swine's flesh and eat very little beef or mutton, and cannot drink tea or coffee, why, dear me, we shall starve to death." In

choco-
late,
cocoa

no meat
in
summer

conversation with one of the brethren the other day, he remarked "the diet of the poor is principally bread and meat, and if they dispense with meat, they will be reduced to very hard fare." I reasoned with him on the subject, and before we had got through, I believe I convinced him that other articles of food could be raised more cheaply and in greater variety than the flesh of animals. But just at the present time we are destitute, to some extent, of this needed variety; and, hence, the very apparent necessity that we as a people should turn our attention to the multiplication of varieties of food in our midst. We should not confine ourselves to a few articles of diet and be content therewith; but the people who have the opportunity of so doing should cultivate a variety of food for the benefit of themselves and families.

variety needed

It is a fact, which the experience of ages has confirmed, that man of all creatures, requires the greatest variety of food. His stomach is fitted to digest a greater variety of food than the stomach of any other animal. God has created him lord of creation, and all that is created around us is created for men's use and benefit. It would therefore be very unwise for intelligent man, inasmuch as God has given to him the vegetable creation, and has made him lord of the animal creation and placed him as monarch of the finny tribes, to be content to sit down and eat as our degraded Indians do.

It is to remedy this that we hear the teachings that are given at the present time by the servants of God. Man requires food to build up his body. He requires food that is adapted to the development of bone, muscle, and sinew; but this is not all. He requires food that is suitable to feed his brain and to supply the waste sustained in consequence of the use of his mental faculties. There is a necessity, therefore, for us to take these things into consideration. My opinion is that it will be most difficult for fathers of families to induce their wives and children to refrain from the use of tea and coffee, if they do not supply their tables with other articles in their place, and unless food, suitable for the requirements of the human system, is provided, our wives and children will be exposed to constant temptation to transgress the counsels that are given in regard to our diet. It is an exceedingly difficult thing for most people to break off and discontinue cherished and long-standing habits. A man who has never drunk tea, coffee, or spirit, or one who has never chewed or smoked tobacco, is not at all affected by the counsel to discontinue their use; but they who have been accustomed to them miss them when they are deprived of them, and they want something to supply their place. I speak, now, not from my own experience, but from waht I have heard others say on these things. There is a craving felt by parties when they discontinue the use of these stimulants, and they need variety. This variety must be supplied, and we must take steps to supply it.

fish
good
for
brain

The culture of fish has been alluded to. Physiologists say that fish contain more of the elements necessary to strengthen and build up the brain than almost any other known substance. It would supply a great want if we had it in abundance. But our supply of this article of food is very limited, and hence we are taught at the present time to take measures for its increase. I see no reason why we should not raise our own fish as we do our eggs or chickens. This Territory is better adapted to the raising of fish, in consequence of our system of irrigation, than any on the Continent we know anything of, and I believe that the time is not far distant when our farmers will raise fish for their own tables as they now raise beef, mutton, pork, fruit or any other article of diet now in use. It can be done easily by bestowing a little attention, thought and care on the subject.

fruit

We must also cultivate fruit more extensively than we now do; and we must multiply every variety of diet, and if it is possible discover new varieties. It is only a few hundred years since the potato was discovered, and what a blessing it has proven to man. There are other vegetables, probably, as good and as healthful as it is if we could only bring them into use. But vegetables are not grown among us as they should be; there is not that attention paid to them that, it seems to me, they should receive. My theory is, that if we wish to raise a healthy, noble looking, intellectual and perfect race of men and women we must feed our children properly. We must prevent the use by them of every article that is hurtful or noxious in its nature. We must not permit them to drink liquor or hot drinks, or hot soups or to use tobacco or other articles that are injurious. I do not believe that you could ever make as great and noble race of men, if you feed them on one article of food alone, as if you gave them a variety of diet. We have illustrations of this in India, where the chief diet is rice—of itself a very good article of food. We have other illustrations in the case of other races. A people who, for instance, are fed on potatoes alone do not have the stamina that they would have if they had a greater variety of food. Such a people could, I believe, be kept subjected more easily to thraldom than a nation which is better fed. The millions of India are kept in subjection by as many thousands of Europeans. There are doubtless many cuases for this, among the chief of which is their diet.

boun-
teous
land

God has given us a land that is bounteous: every variety of food can be produced here in the greatest profusion. It only requires the exercise of the powers with which we are endowed, with proper industry, to bring forth food in the greatest abundance and supply every want of man and beast. But whilst I speak in this strain about a variety of food, I am opposed in my own feelings, to a great variety of food at one meal. I believe that we enslave our women; we crush out their lives by following the pernicious habits of our forefathers in ths respect. We sit down to table, and, especially if we have friends, our tables are covered with every delicacy and variety that we can think of. I believe in variety at different meals, but not at one meal. I do not believe in mixing up our food. This is hurtful. It destroys the stomach by overtaxing the digestive powers; and in addition to that it almost wears out the lives of our

simpli-
city
of
diet

females by keeping them so closely confined over cooking stoves. A variety of food is not incompatible with simplicity of cooking; they can go hand in hand. We can have a variety in diet, and yet have simplicity.

We can have a diet that will be easily prepared, and yet have it healthful. We can have a diet, that will be tasteful, nutritious and delightful to us, and easy to digest; and yet not wear out the lives of our mothers, wives, daughters and sisters in its preparation.

These are topics, my brethren and sisters, that should claim the attention of the Latter-day Saints, because they pertain to our everyday existence here on the earth; and if we follow the course marked out, and seek to follow the counsels given, the result will be that, here in these valleys, we shall raise a race of men who will be the joy of the earth, whose complexions will be like the complexions of angels—full of health, purity, innocence and vitality; men who will live until the wheels of life will stand still in consequence of the gradual decay of the body; not afflicted and brought to the grave prematurely by disease engendered by improper feeding and other unhealthy habits. We can do what no other people ever could do, at least no other people living in the present generation. We are here a new people, forming our habits and laying the foundation of a great work, and of course are in a state of transition. We can therefore, if we so please, accommodate ourselves to new habits—habits recommended and taught to us by the servants of God. One of the great advantages that would result from our having a more simple diet would be that we should be less apt to overload our stomachs through the tempting character of the food we eat. How often is it the case, after we have eaten enough, somebody will say, "Here is something I would like you to eat a little of; do taste it." Well, you taste, and before you are aware of it, you have eaten more than you should; your stomach rebels, and you feel that you have done a wrong, and if your stomachs are weak, you have to pay the penalty of your imprudence.

Vol. XIII, 153-154, 155, by Brigham Young, November 4, 1869:

light
nutri-
tious
break-
fasts

...I told her I wished to get up a society whose members would agree to have a light, nice breakfast in the morning, for themselves and children, without cooking something less than forty different kinds of food, making slaves of themselves and requiring three or four hired girls to wash dishes. Prepare your breakfast something like they do in England, bread and butter, a little cheese, a few eggs, food that is light and nutritious, and which does not require so much labor in cooking, and instead of tea, if you cannot drink cold water, make a bowl of water gruel or meal porridge and you will save dirtying three or four dishes, knives and forks, or spoons, to each individual that sits at the table.

change
diets

This would be something to change your feelings and the fashions of society. Will you do it? If you want something new, try this; and when dinner time comes, don't pile the table full of roast meat, boiled meat and baked meat, fat mutton, beef and pork; and in addition to this two or three kinds of pies and cakes; neither urge the children, the father and every one at the table to eat and gorge themselves till they are so full that when night comes they will want a doctor. This will do for a change.

receive
Spirit

free
from
pains

When we go on a trip to the settlements and stop at the brethren's houses, it is, "Brother Brigham, let us manifest our feelings towards you and your company. I tell them to do so, but give me a piece of johnny-cake; I would rather have it than their pies and tarts and sweetmeats. Let me have something that will sustain nature and leave my stomach and whole system clear to receive the Spirit of the lord and be free from headache and pains of every kind. If I can experience this, it will suit me. What do you say to it, sisters? Do you want a revolution? They want one in France; but you need not go to France to have a revolution of this kind. Yet in that country there are about twenty-four millions who never eat any flesh meat at all.

The Americans, as a nation, are killing themselves with their vices and high living. As much as a man ought to eat in half an hour they swallow in three minutes,

gulping
food

gulping down their food like the canine quadruped under the table, which, when a chunk of meat is thrown to it, swallows it before you can say "twice." If you want a reform, carry out the advice I have just given you. Dispense with your multitudinous dishes, and, depend upon it, you will do much towards preserving your families from sickness, disease and death.

If this method were adopted in this community, I will venture to say that it would add ten years to the lives of our children. That is worth a great deal.

Mothers
instead
of
doctors

...Learn to take proper care of your children. If any of them are sick the cry now, instead of "Go and fetch the Elders to lay hands on my child!" is, "Run for a doctor." Why do you not live so as to rebuke disease? It is your privilege to do so without sending for the Elders. You should go to work to study and see what you can do for the recovery of your children. If a child is taken sick with fever give it something to stay that fever or relieve the stomach and bowels, so that mortification may not set in. Treat the child with prudence and care, with faith

caution
with
medi-
cine

and patience, and be careful in not overcharging it with medicine. If you take too much medicine into the system, it is worse than too much food. But you will always find that an ounce of preventive is worth a pound of cure. Study and learn something for yourselves.

Vol. XIII, 275-278, by Brigham Young, October 30, 1870:

But you put cattle into a field where there is tobacco and you will see that none of them will eat it unless they are sick, they will take it then, but at no other time. If a horse, ox or sheep be in good, ordinary health it will not touch it, and to say that it is necessary for man is absurd! Well, is it good for nothing? Was it created in vain? No, the Word of Wisdom tells us that tobacco is for sick cattle, and the dumb brute will demonstrate this if it is sick and can get at it. The tobacco plant and the lobelia plant are similar in taste and outward appearance, though not in their effects; but the former is for cattle, the latter for man. The difference in their effects is chiefly, that lobelia has no narcotic influence, while tobacco has.

I wish to ask those brethren who are in the habit of using tobacco, Won't you leave it alone and try lobelia, and see if you can become attached to it? If you can, it will prove that it possesses narcotic properties; if you cannot, it will prove that it possesses no such properties. Mankind would not become attached to these unnecessary articles were it not for the poison they contain. The poisonous or narcotic properties in spirits, tobacco and tea are the cause of their being so much liked by those who use them. I hear something occasionally about tea, but I say if the ladies would take the natural leaf from the stem and dry it upon wood they would not become attached to it as they do to the green tea, Young Hyson, Gunpowder and other popular brands, for these kinds are cured on copper, and they partake more or less of the nature of the copper on which they are dried, through being impregnated with its poisonous qualities.

tea cured on copper

I say this to the brethren and sisters, that they may see if they can become attached to and really crave any of these stimulants that do not contain quite a quantity of poison. There is no doubt whatever that the food we eat, and which is absolutely necessary to sustain us, contains poison. I do not dispute that the poison contained in the bread that has been distributed from the table this afternoon, if extracted by a skillful chemist, would be enough to kill; but still, as combined with the other constituent elements of which bread is composed, it is not injurious, and we eat it without harm. But where we find so much poison in articles the people will become very strongly attached to them in a very short time. For instance, how quickly persons become attached to the practice of opium eating; they cannot live without it! if there was no poison in it, it would not operate upon the system as it does. In some countries it is said that the fair sex are in the habit of arsenic eating, and this is for the special purpose of

poison causes addiction

improving the complexion. Let a lady commence taking the smallest possible particle of this article, and if she continues the practice, in a few years she will not be able to live without it.

live
without
or die
without

Many of our sisters think they cannot live without tea. I will tell you what we can do—I have frequently said it to my brethren and sisters—if they cannot live without tea, coffee, brandy, whisky, wine, beer, tobacco, &c., they can die without them. This is beyond controversy. If we had the determination that we should have, we would live without them or die without them. Let the mother impregnate her system with these narcotic influences when she is bringing forth a family on the earth, and what does she do? She lays the foundation of weakness, palpitation of the heart, nervous affections, and many other ills and diseases in the system of her offspring that will afflict them from the cradle to the grave. Is this righteous or unrighteous, good or evil? Let my sisters ask and answer the question for themselves, and the conclusion which each and every one of them may come to is this, "If I do an injury to my child, I sin."

untimely
graves

We very well know that the customs which prevail in the world are such as to cause millions and millions of children to go to untimely graves. Infants, children, youth, young men and young women, thousands and ten thousands of them go to an untimely grave through the diseases engendered in their systems by their progenitors. Is this wrong or is it right? If it is wrong we should abstain from every influence and practice which produces these evil effects; if it is right, then practice them. But we say it is wrong; God says it is wrong, and He has pointed out in a few instances the path for us to walk in, by observing the Word of Wisdom, and He has declared that it is fitted to the capacity of the Saints, yea the weakest of all who are or can be called Saints. And this Word of Wisdom prohibits the use of hot drinks and tobacco. I have heard it argued that tea and coffee are not mentioned therein; that is very true; but what were the people in the habit of taking as hot drinks when that revelation was given? Tea and coffee. We were not in the habit of drinking water very hot, but tea and coffee—the beverages in common use. And the Lord said hot drinks are not good for the body nor the belly, liquor is not good for the body nor the belly, but for the washing of the body, &c. Tobacco is not good, save for sick cattle, and for bruises and sores, its cleansing properties being then very useful.

Vol. XIII, 339, by Joseph F. Smith, November 12, 1870:

chil-
dren
lose
respect

...What will a child, when he begins to reflect, think of a parent who, professing to believe that the Word of Wisdom is part of the Gospel of Jesus Christ, and has been given by revelation, violates it every day of his life? He will grow up to believe that his parent is a hypocrite and without faith in the Gospel.

Vol. XIV, 20, by Brigham Young, May 6, 1870:

Now let us observe the Word of Wisdom. Shall I take a vote on it? Everybody would vote, but who would observe it? A good many, but not all. I can say that a good many do observe their covenants in this thing. But who is it that understands wisdom before God? In some respects we have to define it for ourselves—each for himself—according to our own views, judgment and faith, and the observance of the Word of Wisdom, or the interpretation of God's requirements on this subject, must be left, partially, with the people. We cannot make laws like the Bedes and Persians. We cannot say you shall never drink a cup of tea, or you shall never taste of this, or you shall never taste of that; but we can say that Wisdom is justified of her children.

Vol. XIV, 108-109, by Brigham Young, August 8, 1869:

...If the Saints would be faithful in cultivating these gifts (of healing, of discerning of spirits, of tongues, of the interpretation of tongues, of prophecy, etc.) every doctor might be removed from our midst. Let the mothers, say nothing about the Elders in Israel, exercise the faith that it is their right to exercise, and I am satisfied that nine out of every ten children that now die might be saved. Doctors and their medicines I regard as a deadly bane in any community. Give your children, when sick, a little simple herb drink; and if they have eaten too much let them go without food until their stomachs are cleansed and purified, and have faith in the name of Jesus and in the ordinances of his Church, and they will live. That is my faith with regard to this thing. I am not very partial to doctors and lawyers, I can see no use for them unless it is to raise grain or go to mechanical work. But I need not go into this subject at the present.

Vol. XIV, 212, by George A. Smith, August 13, 1871:

I notice in the observance of the Word of Wisdom, a manifestation of the Holy Spirit connected with it. Whenever a person has failed to observe it, and becomes a slave to his appetite in these simple things, he gradually grows cold in his religion; hence I constantly feel to exhort my brethren and sisters, both by precept and example, to observe the Word of Wisdom. We should not be thoughtless, careless nor neglectful in the observance of its precepts. "Why, it cannot do any hurt," says one, "to take a glass of ale!" I recollect seeing a man once in England, who said to me, "Mr. Smith, how can it be possible that it can injure a man to drink the matter of half a pint of ale?" He had had so much that he could not stand without leaning against a fence, and yet he could not see how it could injure a man to take a half pint; but if he had not taken the first half pint he could have stood as well as anybody. It may as well be said, and no doubt often is, How can it hurt a man to chew tobacco or to drink tea? It injures, because it creates a disturbance in the human organization, and that disturbance, if continued, creates an appetite to which its possessor becomes a slave, and it shortens his days; and while living his condition is such that he cannot as efficiently perform the duties devolving upon him as he otherwise could.

Vol. XV, 225-226, by Brigham Young, October 9, 1872:

doctors   Would you want doctors? Yes, to set bones. We should want a good surgeon for that, or to cut off a limb.

But do you want doctors? For not much of anything else,
let me tell you, only the traditions of the people lead
them to think so; and here is a growing evil in our midst.
It will be so in a little time that not a woman in all Israel
will dare to have a baby unless she can have a doctor by
her. I will tell you what to do, you ladies, when you find
you are going to have an increase, go off into some
country where you cannot call for a doctor, and see if
you can keep it. I guess you will have it, and I guess it
will be all right, too. Now the cry is, "Send for a doctor."
If you have a pain in the head, "Send for a doctor;" if
your heel aches, "I want a doctor;" "my back aches,
and I want a doctor." The study and practice of
anatomy and surgery are very good; they are
mechanical, and are frequently needed. Do you not
think it is necessary to give medicine sometimes? Yes,
but I would rather have a wife of mine that knows what
medicine to give me when I am sick, than all the
professional doctors in the world. Now let me tell you
about doctoring, because I am acquainted with it, and
know just exactly what constitutes a good doctor in
intui-   physic. It is that man or woman who, by revelation, or
tive   we may call it intuitive inspiration, is capable of
inspi-   administering medicine to assist the human system
ration   when it is besieged by the enemy called Disease, but if
they have not that manifestation, they had better let the
sick person alone. I will tell you why: I can see the faces
of the congregation, but I do not see two alike; and if I
could look into your nervous systems and behold the
operations of disease, from the crowns of your heads to
the soles of your feet, I should behold the same
difference that I see in your physiognomy—there would
be no two precisely alike. Doctors make experiments,
and if they find a medicine that will have the desired
effect on one person, they set it down that it is good for
everybody, but it is not so, for upon the second person
that medicine is administered to, seemingly with the
same disease, it might produce death. If you do not
know this, you have not had the experience that I have. I
say that unless a man or woman who administers
medicine to assist the human system to overcome
disease, understands, and has that intuitive knowledge,

by the Spirit, that such an article is good for that
individual at that very time, they had better let him
alone. Let the sick do without eating, take a little of
something to cleanse the stomach, bowels and blood,
natural   and wait patiently, and let Nature have time to gain the
remedies   advantage over the disease. Suppose, for illustration,
we draw a line through this congregation, and place
those on this side where they cannot get a doctor,
without it is a surgeon, for thirty or fifty years to come;
and put the other side in a country full of doctors, and
doctors   they think they ought to have them, and this side of the
vs.   house that has no doctor will be able to buy the
no   inheritance of those who have doctors, and overrun
doctors   them, outreach them, and buy them up, and finally
obliterate them, and they will be lost in the masses of
those who have no doctors. I know what some say when
they look at such things, but that is the fact. Ladies and
gentlemen, you may take any country in the world, I do
not care where you go, and if they do not employ
doctors, you will find they will beat communities that
employ them, all the time. Who is the real doctor? That
man who knows by the Spirit of revelation what ails an
individual, and by the same Spirit knows what medicine
to administer. That is the real doctor, the others are
quacks.

Vol. XVI, 281, by George A. Smith, October 8, 1873:

I spoke here, the other day, a little in relation to the
Word of Wisdom, and I again appeal to my brethren and
my sisters to observe it, for I know that if they neglect to
shorten   do so, before they pass behind the vail they will mourn,
days   wail and weep in their hearts, for it will have a tendency
decrease   to shorten their days, decrease their strength and
strength   lessen their glory. To those brethren who indulge in
lessen   intoxicating drinks I say, Cease this folly. Brethren, I
glory   appeal to you in the name of humanity, in mercy to your
wives and children, in the name of my Father in heaven
and in the name of his Son, and say, Waste not your
strength and your life with folly of this kind. Let
intoxicating drinks alone, entirely alone.

Vol. XVII, 252, 252-253, by George A. Smith, October 11, 1874:

...As a short illustration, and to draw the minds of the congregation directly to the points of instruction, I am disposed to read a portion of the rules of the United Order.

rules
of
United
Order

The third rule is—"We will observe or keep the word of wisdom, according to the spirit and meaning thereof." Remember this, brethren and sisters. I hear occasionally of brethren indulging in intoxicating drinks, and I see many of them yet, even young men, who indulge in the use of tobacco, a habit which is very pernicious and injurious to health, and a violation of the word of wisdom. There are also other violations of this rule among us which should cease, for we are told in the word of wisdom that if we will observe it will all our hearts, keeping the commandments of God, we shall

promise

have faith, health and strength, marrow in our bones, and have wisdom and great treasures of knowledge, and the destroyer will pass by us and not slay us. Brethren, how general it is with us when persons are sick and afflicted, or when our children are sick, to say to the Elders—"Brethren, come and lay your hands upon them," and in thousands of instances they are healed. Perhaps we are losing some of our faith. We read in the Scriptures that King Asa, whom God had healed and blessed, when he was diseased he trusted not to the Lord, but sought physicians, and King Asa died. While we recommend and approve of using every reasonable means within our power to preserve our

first
faith

lives and those of our children, we do depend, first of all, upon faith in the holy Gospel, the administration of its ordinances and the fulfillment of the promises of God; and inasmuch as we observe the word of wisdom and keep the commandments of God we have faith, and we have the promises of God, upon which we can rely, and by which thousands and thousands are delivered from the afflictions which prey upon them.

Vol. XIX, 67-69, by Brigham Young, July 19, 1877:

The first thing I am going to introduce to my sisters is the condition of this community. Since I have come into this place I understand that you have a great deal of sickness here. "It is very warm weather," one says. "A great deal of sickness," says another. I want to say to you that warm weather is very healthy weather. And I can say still further, with regard to our climate, a dry climate is a healthy climate, much more so than where a damp miasma arises from swamps and decayed materials, which is so frequently the case in low lands, especially in the Mississippi Valley, but not so on this western slope. Now I want you to understand what I am talking to you—this weather is beautiful weather to enjoy health.

Now I will talk to you mothers. If I were invited to your houses to take supper, or breakfast to-morrow morning, if you have it within your reach you will have a platter of meat cooked, and will put this before your children. They are hungry, and require something to satisfy the demands of nature. You place this before them, and, if they choose, in our country, they may gorge themselves to overflowing. You do not stop to ask them if they have eaten sufficient, and ask them now to desist, and eat moderately. You will let your children eat green apples and berries of any kind; sit down and eat fat meat, if they choose it and like it; and fill their systems with swine's flesh which is more susceptible of diseases than any other flesh that we eat. It is not like fish or fowl. It is susceptible of disease of every kind, and will impregnate the system with disease far quicker than any other food that we eat. Now, mothers, it is well for you to think of these things. I will tell you how you can enjoy health. You let your children have a little milk in the morning. I would prefer putting it over the fire and boiling it, and put one-third water in it, with a little flour and a particle of salt to make it palatable. Give them a little bread with it—not soft bread, teach your children to eat crust—hard baked bread, that the Americans would call stale, but the English would not. Teach them to eat this, and to eat sparingly. Instead of

sick-
ness

healthy
climate

chil-
dren
eat
wrong

swine
causes
disease

drinking unhealthy water, boil such water, and let it stand until it is cool. If the children are in the least troubled with summer complaint, and are weak in their bowels, make a weak composition tea, sweeten it with loaf sugar, and put a little nice cream in it; and let the children make a practice of drinking composition instead of cold water. Mothers, keep the children from eating meat; and let them eat vegetables that are fully matured, not unripe, and bread that is well baked, not soft. Do not put your loaf into the oven with a fire hot enough to burn it before it is baked through, but with a slow heat, and let it remain until it is perfectly baked; and I would prefer, for my own eating, each and every loaf to be no thicker than my two hands—you tell how thick they are—and I would want the crust as thick as my hand.

ripe vegetables

Now for experience. You see I am creeping up in years; and I have been from my boyhood a person of observation. I have many and many a time said to children when they begged for the soft bread, that was not baked thoroughly, "Look here; you will not live very long; you will probably come to a premature grave." I have noticed that invariably the child that selects the soft bread to be a short-lived person. The children that hunt around after the crust and eat it, I have noticed endure, live, and continue to live on. Have you ever noticed this? I have quite aged sisters here; and I am talking to many that have children, grand-children and great-grand-children, like myself. Have you ever observed this? If you have not I wish you would commence to reflect upon it.

soft bread not good

You say you are improving. These societies are for the improvement of our manners, our dress, our habits, and our methods of living. Now, sisters, will you take notice, and instruct those who are not here to-day, to adopt this rule—stop your children from eating meat, and especially fat meat, let them have composition to drink, instead of unhealthy water; let them eat a little milk porridge; let them eat sparingly and not oppress the stomach so as to create a fever. No matter whether it is a child or a middle-aged person, whenever the

no meat for children

stomach is over-loaded and charged with more than is required it creates a fever; this fever creates sickness, until death relieves the sufferer. Now the people do not think of this. You ought to have thought of it. I have taught this for years and years to the people. When we commence to shape our lives according to the judgment that is given to us, and we exercise a proper portion of thought, and study the laws of life, to know what to give, and how to guide and direct our children and ours, we shall find that the longevity of this people will increase. Although it is a fact that the longevity of this people is as great perhaps as that of any other people at the present time; yet we shall find if we will hearken to the wisdom our Heavenly Father has given us, this will increase; and we shall learn at once that we are enjoying better health, we shall have a greater amount of vitality, and a stronger development of ability, and by temperance and moderation lay the foundation for the development of the mind. Now, here let me throw in a side remark. I do not mean to go without food and go to fasting. This is the other extreme. A sufficient amount of food that will agree with the stomach is healthy, and should be partaken of. Aged or middle aged, youth or children, never should go without food until their stomachs are faint, demanding something to sustain their systems, and continue to undergo this; for this lays the foundation of weakness, and this weakness will tempt disease. But keep the stomach in a perfectly healthy condition.

eat
mode-
rately

Now I do not mean fasting, but eating moderately; and if my sisters will go home and commence to adopt this rule, you will find that you begin to get better, your children and neighbors will get better. We do not expect all to be free from sickness. I have had a great deal of sickness in my life. I do not expect to be free from the ills, the weakness, debility and disease that prey upon the human family, but we can amend our ways, and amend our life by being prudent; and I wish the sisters to understand this, and to adopt these instructions; and if you do not learn before the month of July is gone that your sickness has departed, I shall be very much disappointed. So much for the health of the people. Will you listen?

not
totally
free
from
ills

Vol. XXV, 38-39, by Erastus Snow, October 5, 1883:

Let us remember and ponder upon these counsels, and cleave to the Priesthood and have confidence in it; and let the Elders administer to the sick in faith, and let them rebuke disease when the Spirit prompts them, and it will be rebuked, and the sick will be healed by the power of God. Every Elder in Israel should so live before the Lord as to have confidence in Him to do this. And let the Presidents of Stakes and the Bishops and the leading influential men encourage faith among the people, depending upon God and the ordinances of His house rather than trusting in man. And while they seek for wisdom to nurse the sick in a manner calculated to do them good, let them learn too, that herb medicine, unless administered in wisdom and intelligence, is liable to injure the patient instead of benefitting him. And let the Elders lay aside strong drinks and tobacco, and discontinue the practice of everything having a tendency to injure the system, and set examples before our sons and daughters that is worthy of imitation. If parents will pursue this course they will command the respect of their children; and when the time comes for them to go down to their graves, their children will point to them in affection and pride as being the chief means, under God, of their learning His ways and walking in His paths, and of eschewing those pernicious habits which are wasting away the life of our nation, and that are gradually undermining society and destroying the human race. It is the design of the Almighty to raise up in these mountains a hardy and a healthy people, a people who shall live according to the laws of heaven that govern them, in whom shall be found the elements of faith and power; and it becomes our duty to shape our lives accordingly. And that God may help us to do so, and to accomplish all that is required of us, is my earnest desire and prayer. Amen.

heal
the
sick

caution
with
herbs

Index

Index